Painting Techniques & Projects

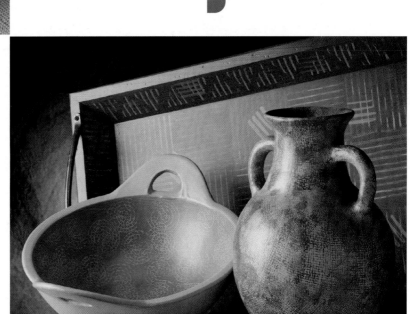

CREATIVE
HOME
ARTS
CLUB

Creative Home Arts Library™

CREDITS

Cover Design, Text and Production: Gina Germ,
Tom Carpenter, Heather Koshiol, Happi Olson

Copyright © Creative Publishing international, Inc.
  2004

President/CEO: Ken Fund
Vice President/Publisher: Linda Ball
Vice President/Retail Sales: Kevin Haas
Executive Editor: Alison Brown Cerier

Printed by:
  R. R. Donnelley
1 2 3 4 5 / 08 07 06 05 04

ISBN 1-58923-214-3

CONTENTS

BRING YOUR HOME TO LIFE WITH *PAINTING TECHNIQUES & PROJECTS!*

Anybody can tape up around the windows and woodwork, cover the furniture, throw down some plastic sheets, and paint a wall or walls. And the end result is fine—a new color, a fresh look, the room even smells brand new for a few weeks.

But there's so much more that can be done with your walls and other home decor items. Don't look at them as problems to be covered and forgotten. Rather, consider them as opportunities for using paint to make your home breathtakingly beautiful!

That's the idea behind *Painting Techniques & Projects*. These pages show you how to bring your home to life, and bring real life to your home! Hundreds of full-color photographs are the keys, guiding you step-by-step through a wide variety of creative painting projects for your walls, furniture and home decor objects. You'll see exactly how to master each painting technique.

To get you started, we present everything you need to know about the tools, brushes, supplies, primers, paints and other materials you will need … and how to use them. Once you understand these basics, you're ready to start creating beauty with paint! Then we proceed to show you how to do just that, staying by your side with clear, helpful guidance every step of the way.

Discover the secrets of combing, rag rolling, texturizing and using glazes. Learn the basics of sponge painting, and creating special effects of all kinds. We even show you how to colorwash walls or wood.

Then see how to create the look of stone and marble without the full price tag! Get all the how-to on making creative enamel, cracked and faux finishes. And master the art of creating designs with paint … from trompe l'oeil to a faux mosaic and other special effects.

Don't settle for plain old painted surfaces. With *Painting Techniques & Projects* to guide you, you can bring your home to life!

CREATIVE
HOME
ARTS
—CLUB—

GETTING STARTED

Primers & Finishes

PRIMERS

Some surfaces must be coated with a primer before the paint is applied. Primers ensure good adhesion of paint and are used to seal porous surfaces so paint will spread smoothly without soaking in. It is usually not necessary to prime a nonporous surface in good condition, such as smooth, unchipped, previously painted wood or wallboard. Many types of water-based primers are available; select one that is suitable for the type of surface you are painting.

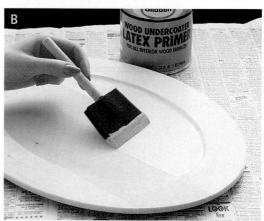

A. FLAT LATEX PRIMER is used for sealing unfinished wallboard. It makes the surface nonporous so fewer coats of paint are needed. This primer may also be used to seal previously painted wallboard before you apply new paint of a dramatically different color. The primer prevents the original color from showing through.

B. LATEX ENAMEL UNDERCOAT is used for priming most raw woods or woods that have been previously painted or stained. A wood primer closes the pores of the wood, for a smooth surface. It is not used for cedar, redwood, or plywoods that contain water-soluble dyes, because the dyes would bleed through the primer.

C. RUST-INHIBITING LATEX METAL PRIMER helps paint adhere to metal. Once a rust-inhibiting primer is applied, water-based paint may be used on metal without causing the surface to rust.

D. POLYVINYL ACRYLIC PRIMER, or PVA, is used to seal the porous surface of plaster and unglazed pottery, if a smooth paint finish is desired. To preserve the texture of plaster or unglazed pottery, apply the paint directly to the surface without using a primer.

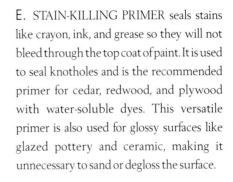

E. STAIN-KILLING PRIMER seals stains like crayon, ink, and grease so they will not bleed through the top coat of paint. It is used to seal knotholes and is the recommended primer for cedar, redwood, and plywood with water-soluble dyes. This versatile primer is also used for glossy surfaces like glazed pottery and ceramic, making it unnecessary to sand or degloss the surface.

FINISHES

Finishes are sometimes used over paint as the final coat. They protect the painted surface with a transparent coating. The degree of protection and durability varies, from a light application of matte aerosol sealer to a glossy layer of clear finish.

F. CLEAR FINISH, such as water-based urethanes and acrylics, may be used over painted finishes for added durability. Available in matte, satin, and gloss, these clear finishes are applied with a brush or sponge applicator. Environmentally safe clear finishes are available in pints, quarts, and gallons (0.5, 0.9, and 3.8 L) at paint supply stores and in 4-oz. and 8-oz. (119 and 237 mL) bottles or jars at craft stores.

G. AEROSOL CLEAR ACRYLIC SEALER, available in matte or gloss, may be used as the final coat over paint as a protective finish. A gloss sealer also adds sheen and depth to the painted finish for a more polished look. Apply aerosol sealer in several light coats rather than one heavy coat, to avoid dripping or puddling. To protect the environment, select an aerosol sealer that does not contain harmful propellants. Use all sealers in a well-ventilated area.

Tools & Supplies

TAPES

When painting, use tape to mask off any surrounding areas. Several brands are available, varying in the amount of tack, how well they release from the surface without damaging the base coat, and how long they can remain in place before removal. You may want to test the tape before applying it to the entire project. The edge of the tape should be sealed tightly to prevent seepage.

PAINT ROLLERS

Paint rollers are used to paint an area quickly with an even coat of paint. Roller pads, available in several nap thicknesses, are used in conjunction with roller frames. Use synthetic or lamb's wool roller pads to apply water-based paints.

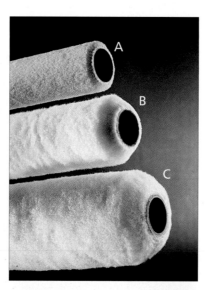

A. SHORT-NAP ROLLER PADS with 1/4" to 3/8" (6 mm to 1 cm) nap are used for applying glossy paints to smooth surfaces like wallboard, wood, and smooth plaster.

B. MEDIUM-NAP ROLLER PADS with 1/2" to 3/4" (1.3 to 2 cm) nap are used as all-purpose pads. They give flat surfaces a slight texture.

C. LONG-NAP ROLLER PADS with 1" to 1 1/4" (2.5 to 3.2 cm) nap are used to cover textured areas in fewer passes.

D. ROLLER FRAME is the metal arm and handle that holds the roller pad in place. A wire cage supports the pad in the middle. Select a roller frame with nylon bearings so it will roll smoothly and a threaded end on the handle so you can attach an extension pole.

E. EXTENSION POLE has a threaded end that screws into the handle of a roller frame. Use an extension pole when painting ceilings, high wall areas, and floors.

PAINTBRUSHES & APPLICATORS

Several types of paintbrushes and applicators are available, designed for various purposes. Select the correct one to achieve the best quality in the paint finish.

A. SYNTHETIC-BRISTLE paintbrushes are generally used with water-based latex and acrylic paints, while B. NATURAL-BRISTLE brushes are used with alkyd, or oil-based paints. Natural-bristle paintbrushes may be used with water-based paints to create certain decorative effects.

C. BRUSH COMBS remove dried or stubborn paint particles from paintbrushes and align the bristles so they dry properly. To use a brush comb, hold the brush in a stream of water as you pull the comb several times through the bristles from the base to the tips. Use mild soap on the brush, if necessary, and rinse well. The curved side of the tool can be used to remove paint from the roller pad.

Stencil brushes are available in a range of sizes. Use the small brushes for fine detail work in small stencil openings, and the large brushes for larger openings. Either D. SNYTHETIC or E. NATURAL-BRISTLE stencil brushes may be used with acrylic paints.

Artist's brushes are available in several types, including F. FAN, G. LINER, and H. FLAT BRUSHES. After cleaning the brushes, always reshape the head of the brush by stroking the bristles with your fingers. Store artist's brushes upright on their handles or lying flat so there is no pressure on the bristles.

I. SPONGE APPLICATORS are used for a smooth application of paint on flat surfaces.

J. PAINT EDGERS with guide wheels are used to apply paint next to moldings, ceilings, and corners. The guide wheels can be adjusted for proper alignment of the paint pad.

Preparing the Surface

To achieve a high-quality and long-lasting paint finish that adheres well to the surface, it is important to prepare the surface properly so it is clean and smooth. The preparation steps vary, depending on the type of surface you are painting. Often it is necessary to apply a primer to the surface before painting it. For more information about primers, refer to pages 8 and 9.

PREPARING SURFACES FOR PAINTING

SURFACE TO BE PAINTED	PREPARATION STEPS	PRIMER
UNFINISHED WOOD	1. Sand surface to smooth it. 2. Wipe with damp cloth to remove grit. 3. Apply primer.	Latex enamel undercoat.
PREVIOUSLY PAINTED WOOD	1. Clean surface to remove any grease and dirt. 2. Rinse with clear water; allow to dry. 3. Sand surface lightly to degloss and smooth it and to remove any loose paint chips. 4. Wipe with damp cloth to remove grit. 5. Apply primer to any areas of bare wood.	Not necessary, except to touch up areas of bare wood; then use latex enamel undercoat.
PREVIOUSLY VARNISHED WOOD	1. Clean surface to remove any grease and dirt. 2. Rinse with clear water; allow to dry. 3. Sand surface to degloss it. 4. Wipe with damp cloth to remove grit. 5. Apply primer.	Latex enamel undercoat.
UNFINSHED WALLBOARD	1. Dust with hand broom, or vacuum with soft brush attachment. 2. Apply primer.	Flat latex primer.
PREVIOUSLY PAINTED WALLBOARD	1. Clean surface to remove any grease and dirt. 2. Rinse with clear water; allow to dry. 3. Apply primer, only if making a dramatic color change.	Not necessary, except when painting over dark or strong color; then use flat latex primer.
UNPAINTED PLASTER	1. Sand any flat surfaces as necessary. 2. Dust with hand broom, or vacuum with soft brush attachment.	Polyvinyl acrylic primer.
PREVIOUSLY PAINTED PLASTER	1. Clean surface to remove any grease and dirt. 2. Rinse with clear water; allow to dry thoroughly. 3. Fill any cracks with spackling compound. 4. Sand surface to degloss it.	Not necessary, except when painting over dark or strong color; then use polyvinyl acrylic primer.
UNGLAZED POTTERY	1. Dust with brush, or vacuum with soft brush attachment. 2. Apply primer.	Polyvinyl acrylic primer or gesso.
GLAZED POTTERY, CERAMIC & GLASS	1. Clean surface to remove any grease and dirt. 2. Rinse with clear water; allow to dry thoroughly. 3. Apply primer.	Stain-killing primer.
METAL	1. Clean surface with vinegar or lacquer thinner to remove any grease and dirt. 2. Sand surface to degloss it and to remove any rust. 3. Wipe with damp cloth to remove grit. 4. Apply primer.	Rust-inhibiting latex metal primer.
FABRIC	1. Prewash fabric without fabric softener to remove any sizing, if fabric is washable. 2. Press fabric as necessary.	None.

Water-based Paints

A wide variety of paint is available from paint supply stores and craft stores. Each type has advantages that make it especially suitable for certain kinds of painting. All of the following are water-based, making cleanup easy with soap and water. Water-based paints are also safer for the environment than oil-based paints.

LATEX PAINTS

Latex paint is fast drying and durable. In addition to the wide range of premixed colors, latex paint can be custom-mixed by a paint professional. It is available in various finishes, from flat latex for a matte appearance to high-gloss latex with maximum sheen. Low-luster latex enamel paint, sometimes referred to as eggshell enamel, has some sheen and provides good coverage; semigloss has a bit more sheen. The glossier the paint, the more durable it is. Packaged in pints, quarts, and gallons (0.5, 0.9, and 3.8 L), latex paint is suitable for general use in small and large jobs.

Latex paint contains acrylic or vinyl resins or a combination of both. Latex paints of acrylic resins are the highest quality, with vinyl-acrylic blends next in quality, followed by paints consisting solely of vinyl resins. High-quality paints may cost significantly more, but they provide an even, complete coverage and wear longer.

CRAFT ACRYLIC PAINT

Craft acrylic paint contains 100 percent acrylic resins. Generally sold in 2-oz., 4-oz., and 8-oz. (59, 119, and 237 mL) bottles or jars, these premixed acrylics have a creamy brushing consistency and give excellent coverage. They should not be confused with the thicker artist's acrylics used for canvas paintings. Craft acrylic paint can be diluted with water, acrylic extender, or latex paint conditioner (page 16) if a thinner consistency is desired. Craft acrylic paints are available in many colors and in metallic, fluorescent, and iridescent formulas.

CERAMIC PAINTS

Ceramic paints provide a scratch-resistant and translucent finish. They can be heat-hardened in a low-temperature oven to improve their durability, adhesion, and water resistance. Latex and acrylic paints may also be used for painting ceramics, provided the surface is properly primed (page 13).

FABRIC PAINTS

Fabric paints have been formulated specifically for painting on fabric. To prevent excessive stiffness in the painted fabric, avoid a heavy application; the texture of the fabric should show through the paint. Once the paints are heat-set with an iron, the fabric can be machine washed and dry-cleaned. Acrylic paints can also be used for fabric painting; textile medium may be added to the acrylics to make them more pliable on fabric.

Paint Mediums

Paint mediums, such as conditioners, extenders, and thickeners, are often essential for successful results in decorative painting. Available in latex or acrylic, paint mediums are formulated to create certain effects or to change a paint's performance without affecting its color. Some mediums are added directly to the paint, while others are used simultaneously with paint. Mediums are especially useful for latex and acrylic paint glazes (page 21), in that they make an otherwise opaque paint somewhat translucent.

LATEX PAINT CONDITIONER, such as Floetrol®, was developed for use in a paint sprayer with latex paint, but this useful product is also essential in making paint glaze for faux finishes. When paint conditioner is added to paint, it increases the drying or "open" time and extends the wet-edge time to avoid the look of overlapping. The mixture has a lighter consistency and produces a translucent paint finish. Latex paint conditioner may be added directly to either latex or acrylic paint.

TEXTILE MEDIUM is formulated for use with acrylic paint, to make it more suitable for fabric painting. Mixed into the paint, it allows the paint to penetrate the natural fibers of cottons, wools, and blends, creating permanent, washable painted designs. After the fabric is painted, it is heat-set with an iron.

ACRYLIC PAINT EXTENDER thins the paint, increases the open time, and makes paint more translucent.

ACRYLIC PAINT THICKENER increases the drying time of the paint while it thickens the consistency. Thickener can be mixed directly into either acrylic or latex paint. Small bubbles may appear while mixing, but they will disappear as the paint mixture is applied. Thickener is used for painting techniques that require a paint with more body, such as combing.

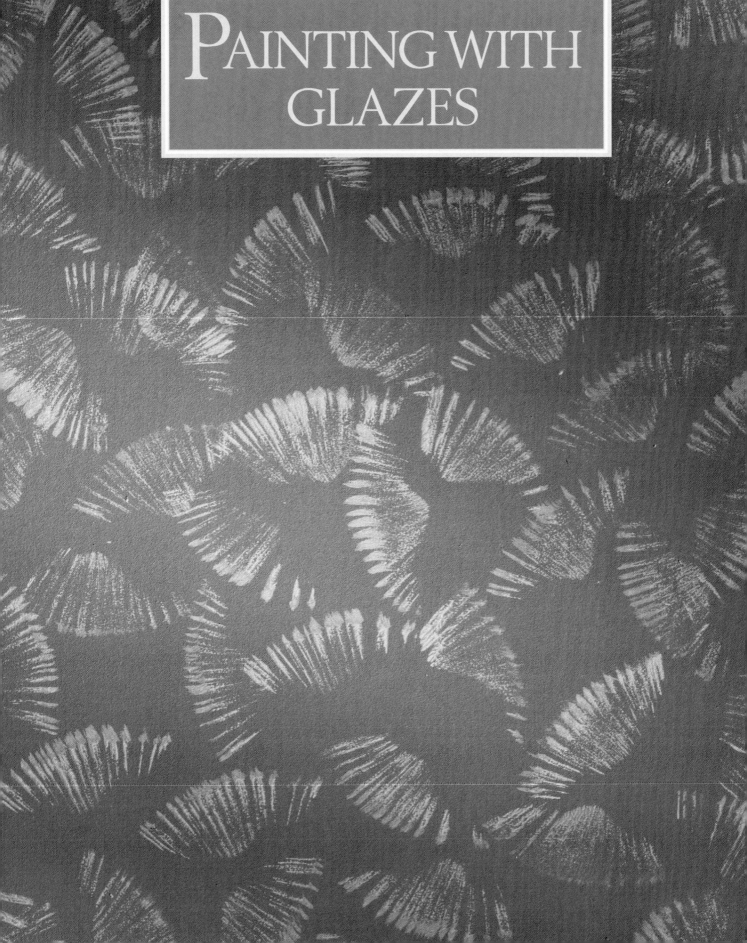

PAINTING WITH GLAZES

Paint Glaze Basics

Many types of decorative painting require the use of a paint glaze, made by adding paint conditioner (page 16) or paint thickener (page 17) to the paint. With these paint mediums, the drying time of the paint is extended, allowing the additional time needed to manipulate the paint before it sets. The glaze has a creamy texture when wet and forms a translucent top coat once it dries.

Paint glazes have traditionally been made from oil-based paints. These oil glazes are messy to use, difficult to clean up, and noxious. Water-based latex and acrylic glazes, on the other hand, are easier to use, safer for the user and the environment, and lower in cost.

The basic glaze (below) is used for several types of decorative painting, including strié, combing, rag rolling, texturizing, and, sometimes, sponging. The glaze is varied slightly for color washing. Without the use of paint glazes, all of these finishes would be nearly impossible to achieve.

TIPS FOR USING PAINT GLAZE

PROTECT the surrounding area with a drop cloth or plastic sheet and wear old clothing, because working with glaze can be messy.

USE wide painter's tape (page 10) to mask off the surrounding surfaces. Firmly rub the edges of the tape, to ensure that the glaze will not seep under it.

USE a paint roller to apply the glaze when even coverage is desired or when painting a large surface, such as a wall.

USE a paintbrush to apply the glaze when a paint finish with more variation and pattern in the surface is desired or when painting a small item.

USE a sponge applicator to apply the glaze when smooth coverage is desired or when painting a small item.

MANIPULATE the glaze while it is still wet. Although humidity affects the setting time, the glaze can usually be manipulated for a few minutes.

WORK with an assistant when using glaze on a large surface. While one person applies the glaze, the other can manipulate it.

BASIC GLAZE

Mix together the following ingredients:

One part latex or craft acrylic paint in desired sheen.

One part latex paint conditioner, such as Floetrol®.

One part water.

How to apply a strié paint finish

MATERIALS

- Low-luster latex enamel in desired color, for the base coat.
- Latex paint in desired sheen and color, for the glaze.
- Latex paint conditioner, such as Floetrol®.
- Wide natural-bristle brush.
- Soft natural-bristle paintbrush.

1. Prepare the surface (page 13). Apply base coat of low-luster latex enamel; allow to dry. Mix the glaze (page 21); apply over base coat in a vertical section about 18" (46 cm) wide, using paint roller or natural-bristle paintbrush.

2. Drag a dry, wide natural-bristle paintbrush through wet glaze, immediately after glaze is applied; work from top to bottom in full, continuous brush strokes. To keep brush rigid, hold bristles of brush against surface with handle tilted slightly toward you. Repeat until desired effect is achieved.

3. Wipe the paintbrush occasionally on clean, dry rag to remove excess glaze, for a uniform strié look. Or rinse brush in clear water, and wipe dry.

4. Brush the surface lightly after the glaze has dried for about 5 minutes, if softer lines are desired; use a soft natural-bristle brush, and keep brush stokes in the same direction as streaks.

Strié

Strié is a series of irregular streaks in a linear pattern, created by using a paint glaze. Especially suitable for walls, this painting technique can also be used for furniture pieces with flat surfaces.

For large surfaces, it is helpful to work with an assistant. After one person has applied the glaze, the other person brushes through the glaze before it dries, to achieve the strié effect. If you are working alone, limit yourself to smaller sections, if possible, since the glaze must be wet to create this look. If it is necessary to interrupt the process, stop only when a section is completed.

Because it can be messy to apply a strié finish, wear old clothing and protect the surrounding area with drop cloths and wide painter's tape. Firmly rub the edges of the tape, to ensure that the glaze will not seep under it.

Strié lends itself well to tone-on-tone colorations, such as ivory over white or tones of blue, although the color selection is not limited to this look. To become familiar with the technique and test the colors, first apply the finish to a sheet of cardboard, such as mat board.

How to apply a combed paint finish

(page 13)

MATERIALS

- Low-luster latex enamel paint in desired color, for base coat.

- Latex paint or craft acrylic paint in desired sheen and color, for glaze.

- Latex paint conditioner, for basic glaze; or acrylic paint thickener, for thickened glaze.

- Paintbrush, paint roller, or sponge applicator.

- Combing tool, opposite.

- Clear finish or aerosol clear acrylic sealer, optional.

1. Prepare the surface (page 13). Apply a base coat of low-luster latex enamel to surface, using a sponge applicator, paintbrush, or paint roller. Allow to dry.

2. Mix basic glaze (page 21) or thickened glaze (opposite); apply to small area at a time, using a sponge applicator, paintbrush, or paint roller. Drag combing tool through wet glaze to create pattern. Allow to dry. Apply clear finish or sealer, if desired.

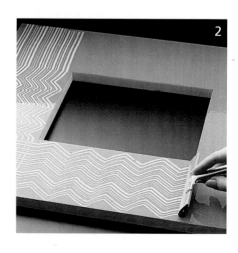

Combing

Combing is a decorative painting technique that has been used for many years, as is evident by the number of antiques with this finish. For this technique, a paint glaze is applied over a base coat of paint. Narrow lines or stripes in the finish are created as you drag the teeth of a comb through the paint glaze, removing some of the glaze to reveal the base coat of paint. For a pronounced effect, the color of the paint glaze may contrast with that of the base coat.

A variety of combed patterns, such as wavy lines, scallops, crisscrosses, zigzags, and basket weaves, can be created. If you are unsatisfied with a particular pattern, the glaze can be wiped off while it is still wet, then reapplied; or the wet glaze can be smoothed out with a paintbrush, then combed into a different pattern.

You may use either the basic paint glaze (page 21) or a thickened glaze of two parts paint and one part acrylic paint thickener. The basic glaze produces a more translucent look and works well on walls and other surfaces without adding texture to the surface. The thickened glaze gives an opaque look with more distinct lines and texture.

A. RUBBER OR METAL COMBING TOOLS, available at craft and art stores, work well for this paint finish. If desired, you can make your own comb by cutting V grooves into a B. RUBBER SQUEEGEE or C. PIECE OF MAT BOARD.

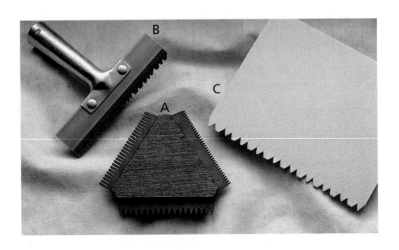

Rag Rolling

Rag rolling is a painting technique that gives a rich, textural look with an allover mottled effect. It works well for walls and other flat surfaces, such as dresser tops and drawers, shelves, bookends, and doors. The basic paint glaze on page 21 can be used in either of the two techniques for rag rolling, *ragging-on* and *ragging-off.*

In ragging-on, a rag is saturated in the prepared paint glaze, wrung out, rolled up, and then rolled across a surface that has been base-coated with low-luster latex enamel paint. Rag-on a single application of glaze over the base coat, for a bold pattern. Or, for a more subtle, blended look, rag-on two or more applications of glaze.

In ragging-off, apply a coat of paint glaze over the base coat, using a paintbrush or paint roller; then roll up a rag and roll it over the wet glaze to remove some of the glaze. This process may be repeated for more blending, but you must work fast, because the glaze dries quickly.

If you are using the ragging-off method on large surfaces, such as walls, it is helpful to have an assistant. After one person applies the glaze, the second person can rag-off the area before the glaze dries. While it is not necessary to complete the entire room in one session, it is important that you complete an entire wall.

With either method, test the technique and the colors that you intend to use on a large piece of cardboard, such as mat board, before you start the project. Generally, a lighter color is used for the base coat, with a darker color for the glaze.

Feel free to experiment with the technique as you test it, perhaps rag rolling two different glaze colors over the base coat. Or try taping off an area, such as a border strip, and rag rolling a second or third color within the taped area.

Because the glaze can be messy to work with, apply a wide painter's tape around the area to be painted and use drop cloths to protect the surrounding surfaces. Wear old clothes and rubber gloves, and keep an old towel nearby to wipe your hands after you wring out the rags.

How to apply a rag-rolled paint finish using the ragging-on method

MATERIALS

◆ Low-luster latex enamel paint, for base coat.

◆ Latex or craft acrylic paint and latex paint conditioner, for glaze; 1 qt. (0.9 L) of each is sufficient for the walls of a 12 ft. x 14 ft. (3.7 x 4.33 m) room.

◆ Paint pail; rubber gloves; old towel; lint-free rags, about 24″ (61 cm) square.

1. Prepare surface (page 13). Apply a base coat of low-luster latex enamel, using paint-brush or paint roller. Allow to dry.

2. Mix basic glaze (page 21) in pail. Dip lint-free rag into glaze, saturating entire rag; wring out well. Wipe excess glaze from hands with old towel.

3. Roll up the rag irregularly; then fold in half to a width equal to both hands.

4. Roll the rag over surface, working upward at varying angles. Rewet rag whenever necessary, and wring out.

5. Repeat the application, if more coverage is desired.

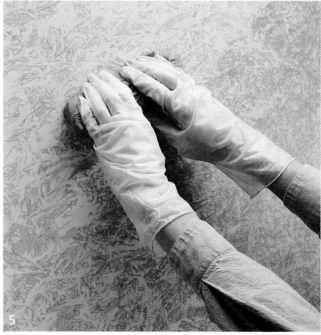

How to apply a rag-rolled paint finish using the ragging-off method

1. Apply base coat of low-luster latex enamel, using paintbrush or paint roller. Allow to dry.

2. Mix basic glaze (page 21); pour into a paint tray. Apply the glaze over the base coat, using paint roller or paint pad.

3. Roll up lint-free rag irregularly; fold in half to width of both hands. Roll the rag through the wet glaze, working upward at varying angles.

COLOR EFFECTS

As shown in the examples below, the color of the base coat is not affected when the ragging-on method is used. With the ragging-off method, the color of the base coat is changed, because the glaze is applied over the entire surface, and then some glaze is removed with a rag to soften the background.

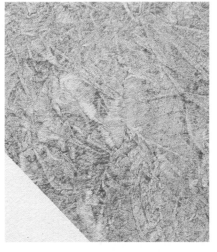

RAGGING-ON is used, applying aqua glaze over a white base coat. The white base coat remains unchanged.

RAGGING-OFF is used, applying aqua glaze over a white base coat. The white base coat is covered with the glaze, then appears as a lighter aqua background when some of the glaze is removed.

RAGGING-ON AND RAGGING-OFF are both used. First a taupe glaze is ragged-on over a white base coat. Then a rust glaze is ragged-off, changing the white base coat to a lighter shade of rust.

Texturizing

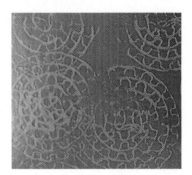

In addition to the methods for strié, combing, and rag rolling, numerous household items and painting supplies can be used with paint glaze to achieve finishes that have visual texture. Rolled or bent pieces of corrugated cardboard cheesecloth, crumpled paper, raffia, plastic wrap, carved potatoes, and scrub brushes create interesting textured effects. The list of items is as endless as your imagination.

For these finishes, use the basic glaze and instructions on page 21. You may apply a coat of glaze directly to the surface, then manipulate it or partially remove it by dabbing the glaze with the item or items you have selected. Or using the alternate method, the glaze may be applied to the selected items, then printed onto the surface. To become familiar with the methods and determine which effects you prefer, experiment with both methods, using a variety of items.

Apply a base coat of paint, using a good-quality low-luster latex enamel, before you apply the glaze. The base coat and the glaze may be in contrasting colors, such as emerald green over white. For a more subtle look, try a tone-on-tone effect, such as two shades of blue, or choose colors that are similar in intensity, such as deep red over deep purple. For even more possibilities, the process can be repeated, using one or more additional colors of glaze. This adds even more visual interest and is especially suitable for small accessories.

LEFT: ACCESSORIES have a variety of textural effects, created using folded cheesecloth for the vase, rolled corrugated cardboard for the bowl, and single-face corrugated cardboard for the tray.

MATERIALS

- Low-luster latex enamel paint in desired color, for base coat.
- Latex or acrylic paint in desired sheen and color, for glaze.
- Latex paint conditioner, such as Floetrol®.
- Items selected for creating the textural effect.

How to apply a texturized paint finish

1. Prepare surface (page 13). Apply a base coat of low-luster latex enamel, using sponge applicator, paintbrush, or paint roller. Allow to dry.

2. Mix glaze (page 21). Apply glaze to a small area at a time, using sponge applicator, paintbrush, or paint roller. A heavier coat of glaze gives a more opaque finish, and a light coat, a more translucent finish.

3. Texturize glaze by dabbing, rolling, or dragging items in the glaze to create patterns; rotate item, if desired, to vary the look. Replace the item as necessary, or wipe the excess glaze from item occasionally.

ALTERNATE METHOD. Follow step 1, above. Then apply glaze to selected item, using a sponge applicator, paintbrush, or paint roller; blot on paper towel or cardboard. Dab, roll, or drag glaze-covered item over base coat, to apply glaze to surface randomly or in desired pattern.

Texturizing techniques

CARDBOARD. Rolled corrugated cardboard is secured by taping it together. Use corrugated end to make design in coat of wet glaze (A). Or apply glaze directly to cardboard; blot, and print designs on surface (B).

Single-face corrugated cardboard is cut to the desired shape. To make design, press corrugated side in coat of wet glaze (C). Or apply glaze directly to corrugated side; blot, and print designs on surface (D).

Continued

Texturizing techniques

CHEESECLOTH. Fold cheesecloth into a flat pad and press into coat of wet glaze (A). Or apply glaze directly to a folded flat pad of cheesecloth, then imprint the cheesecloth onto the surface (B).

PAPER. Crumple paper and press into coat of wet glaze (C). Or apply glaze directly to paper; press onto the surface, crumpling the paper (D).

PLASTIC WRAP. Wrinkle plastic wrap slightly and place over coat of wet glaze; press lightly, and peel off (A). Or apply glaze directly to plastic wrap. Then place plastic wrap on the surface, folding and crinkling it; peel off (B).

FAN BRUSH. Press brush into wet glaze, making uniform rows of fan-shaped impressions (C). Or apply glaze directly to fan brush, and print fan-shaped designs on surface (D).

Continued

Texturizing techniques

(CONTINUED)

COARSE FABRIC. Fanfold a narrow length of burlap or other coarse fabric into a thick pad; apply glaze. Flip folds to back of pad as they become saturated, exposing fresh fabric for texturizing (A). Or, crumple a piece of coarse fabric into loose, irregular folds; apply glaze. Recrumple or start with a fresh piece as fabric becomes saturated (B).

TWINE OR STRING. To texturize with a distinctive pattern, use the twine or string as it comes in a ball. Apply glaze; press onto surface, turning ball or unwinding twine or string as areas become saturated (C). Or, wind string or twine erratically into a tangle for more irregularly shaped pattern (D). Apply glaze and press onto surface.

COARSE NETTING (A). Apply glaze to netting balls, such as those found in bath shops; press onto surface. Netting will not absorb the glaze, so will not become saturated.

SPATTERING (B). Protect the work surface with drop cloths. Mix paints in small cups, combining two parts paint with one part water. Dip tip of brush into paint; remove excess paint on edge of cup. Hold stick and brush over project; strike brush handle against stick to spatter paint. Work from top to bottom in wide strips. Allow first color of paint to dry. Repeat steps for each color, as desired.

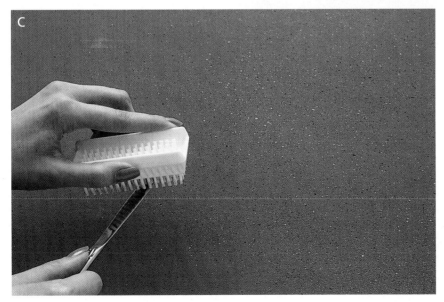

SPECKING (C). Dip ends of stiff-bristled brush into thinned paint. Tap brush onto piece of paper to remove excess paint. Hold brush over surface to be painted; flick bristles toward you using knife or finger, spraying paint away from you. The closer to the surface the brush is held, the finer the spattering and the more control you have.

More ideas for painting with glazes

LEFT: GLAZE FINISHES (page 21) are combined to decorate this small jewelry box. The top and sides of the box are sponge painted; from top to bottom, the drawers are painted using the ragging-on, texturizing, and combing techniques.

CENTER: SPECIALTY PAINT ROLLER quickly creates visual texture on a fabric surface. The roller can be used on hard surfaces, as well.

RIGHT: COMBED SURFACE emphasizes the unique shape of this vase.

Continued

TOP: RAG ROLLING adds textural interest to walls, furniture, and accessories. This tabletop was painted by ragging-off.

LEFT: MAGAZINE RACK is painted by applying two colors of paint, using the ragging-on method (page 28). A final coat of aerosol clear acrylic sealer adds luster and provides a durable finish.

OPPOSITE: VISUAL TEXTURE was applied to this wall, using crumpled burlap.

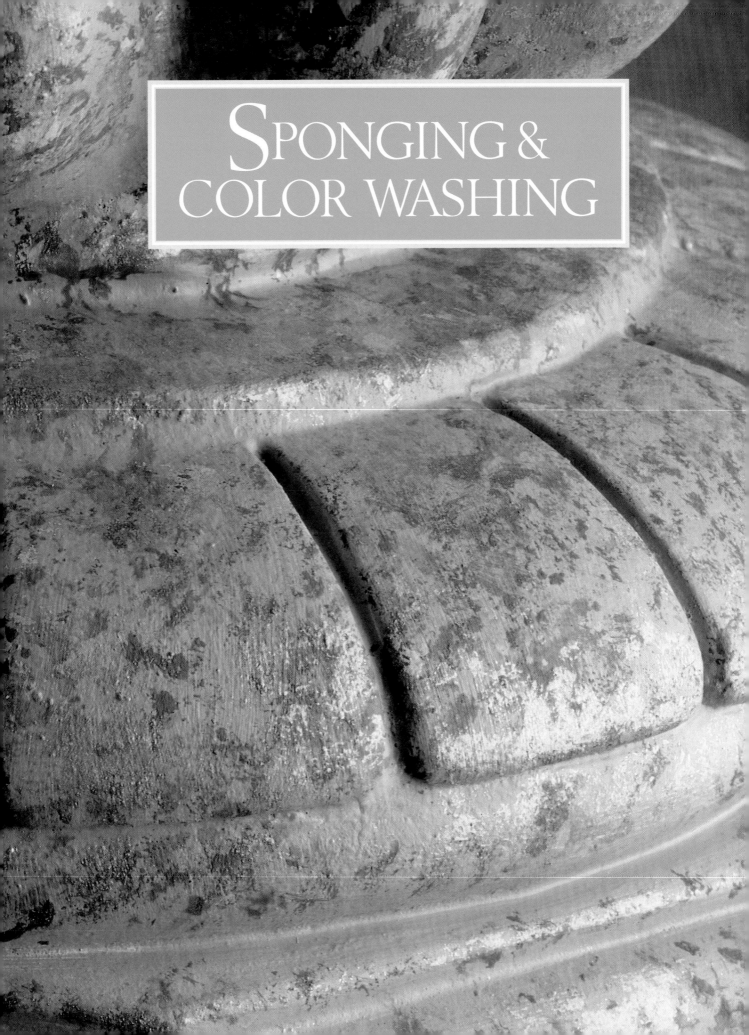

SPONGING & COLOR WASHING

*S*ponge Painting

Sponge painting produces a soft, mottled effect and is one of the easiest techniques to use. To achieve this paint finish, use a natural sea sponge to dab paint onto a surface. Cellulose or synthetic sponges should not be used because they tend to leave identical impressions with hard, defined edges.

The sponged look can be varied, depending on the number of paint colors applied, the sequence in which you apply the colors, and the distance between the sponge impressions. You can use semigloss, low-luster, or flat latex paint for the base coat and the sponging. Or for a translucent finish, use a paint glaze that consists of paint, paint conditioner, and water; make the glaze as on page 21.

To create stripes, borders, or panels, use painter's masking tape to mask off the desired areas of the surface after the first color of sponged paint is applied. Then apply another color to the unmasked areas.

Fabric may be sponge painted, using fabric paint (page 15) or craft acrylic paint mixed with textile medium (page 17). Prewash fabric to remove any sizing, if fabric is washable, and press well to remove wrinkles. Apply paint with sea sponge, as in step 2 on page 46, but do not blot with a wet sponge. When the fabric is dry, heat-set the paint using a dry iron and a press cloth.

How to sponge paint

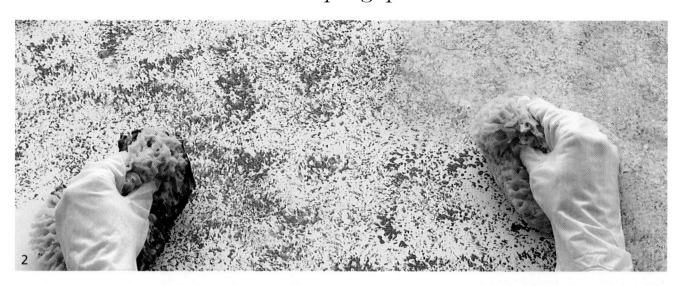

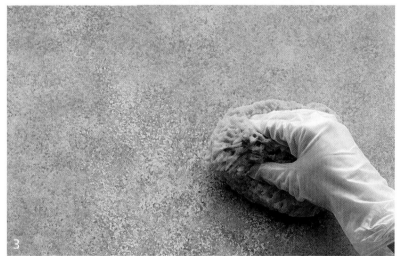 

MATERIALS

◆ Craft acrylic or latex paints in desired sheens and colors, for base coat and for sponging.

◆ Natural sea sponge.

◆ Painter's masking tape.

◆ Carpenter's level, for painting stripes, borders, or panels.

1. Prepare surface (page 13). Apply base coat of desired color. Allow to dry. Rinse sea sponge in water to soften it; squeeze out most of the water. Saturate sponge with paint or with paint glaze (page 21). Blot the sponge lightly on paper towel.

2. Press sponge repeatedly onto surface, as shown at left; work quickly in small areas, and change position of sponge often. Blot paint on surface immediately, using wet sea sponge in other hand, as shown at right; this causes the paint to bleed, for a softened, blended look. Some of the paint is removed with the wet sponge.

3. Continue to apply the first paint color to entire project, blotting with moist sponge. Repeat steps with one or more additional colors of paint, if desired. Allow paint to dry between colors.

4. Optional feathering. Apply final color of paint, using a light, sweeping motion instead of dabbing.

How to sponge paint stripes, borders, or panels

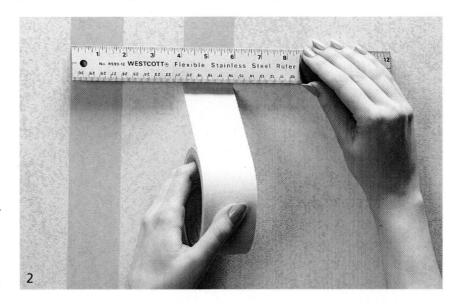

1 Follow steps 1 to 3, opposite. Allow paint to dry thoroughly. Mark light plumb line, using a pencil and carpenter's level. Position first row of painter's masking tape along this line.

2. Measure and position remaining rows of painter's masking tape to mark stripes, borders, or panel areas.

3. Apply second paint color to the unmasked areas of the surface. Allow paint to dry.

4. Remove the painter's masking tape, revealing two variations of sponge painting.

COLOR EFFECTS

When related colors are used for sponge painting, such as two warm colors or two cool colors, a harmonious look is achieved. For a bolder and more unexpected look, sponge paint in a combination of warm and cool colors.

WARM COLORS like yellow and orange blend together for an exciting effect.

COOL COLORS like green and blue blend together for a tranquil effect.

WARM AND COOL COLORS like yellow and blue combine boldly, but sponge painting softens the effect.

Sponge Painting a Check Design

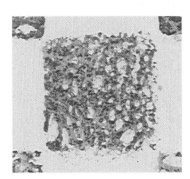

For a dramatic check pattern on walls, apply paint with squares of cellulose sponge. For easier application of the paint, glue the sponge to a piece of plywood and use it as a stamp. As a final step, add more dimension and color to the design, if desired, by lightly stamping another paint color over the checks. For this second paint color, use a square stamp of the same size, or make a stamp in a smaller size or shape.

For even rows, the check pattern works best for walls that have squared corners and ceiling lines. A plumb line may be used as a vertical guide. Plan to start painting at the most prominent corner of the room and work in both directions so full squares will meet at that corner. You may want to divide the dominant wall evenly into checks across the width of the wall.

Flat latex or low-luster latex enamel paint may be used for painting walls. To provide a more durable finish on cabinets and furniture, use a gloss enamel.

How to sponge paint a check design

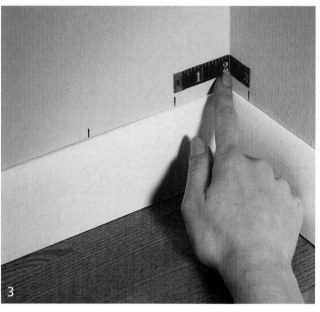

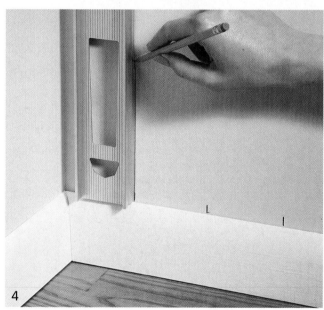

MATERIALS

- Latex paint in desired background color, for base coat.

- Latex paint in one or more colors, for stamped design.

- Large cellulose sponges.

- Scraps of ¼" (6 mm) plywood; hot glue gun and glue sticks.

- Thin transparent Mylar® sheets.

1. Cut cellulose sponge into the desired size of square for check design; cut plywood to same size. Make a stamp by securing sponge to plywood, using hot glue. Make one stamp for each color and shape in design.

2. Prepare surface (page 13). Apply base coat of paint in desired background color; allow to dry. Mark placement for first row of design, at bottom of wall, using pencil. For example, for a 3" (7.5 cm) stamp, lightly mark wall at 3" (7.5 cm) intervals. (Pencil markings are exaggerated to show detail.)

3. Mark the wall to corner. If full width of the design does not fit into the corner, measure around corner, and mark. Then continue marking full widths. Mark spaces on all walls.

4. Lightly mark a plumb line on wall, at the first marking from corner, using a level and pencil. Or hang a string at corner, using a pushpin near top of wall; weight string at bottom so it acts as a plumb line.

5. Apply paint to the sponge, using paintbrush. Stamp the bottom row of checks onto the wall.

6. Continue to stamp rows of checks, working up from bottom of wall and using previous row and plumb line as horizontal and vertical guides. If full stamped design does not fit into corners or at top of wall, leave area unpainted at this time.

7. Allow paint to dry. To fill in areas with partial stamped designs, place a piece of Mylar over previously painted checks to protect wall. Stamp design up to corners and top of wall, overlapping stamp onto Mylar. Allow paint to dry.

8. Add dimension and color to check design, if desired, using stamp of same size and shape as checks, or cut to a different size and shape. Apply another paint color, stamping very lightly over painted checks. Dispose of used stamps.

More ideas for sponge painting

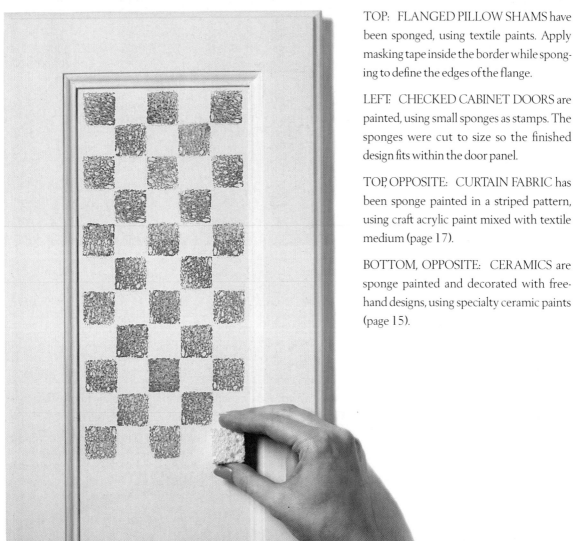

TOP: FLANGED PILLOW SHAMS have been sponged, using textile paints. Apply masking tape inside the border while sponging to define the edges of the flange.

LEFT: CHECKED CABINET DOORS are painted, using small sponges as stamps. The sponges were cut to size so the finished design fits within the door panel.

TOP, OPPOSITE: CURTAIN FABRIC has been sponge painted in a striped pattern, using craft acrylic paint mixed with textile medium (page 17).

BOTTOM, OPPOSITE: CERAMICS are sponge painted and decorated with free-hand designs, using specialty ceramic paints (page 15).

*C*olor-washed Walls

Color washing is an easy paint finish that gives walls a translucent, watercolored look. It adds visual texture to flat drywall surfaces, and it further emphasizes the already textured surface of a plaster or stucco wall.

In this technique, a color-washing glaze is applied in a cross-hatching fashion over a base coat of low-luster latex enamel, using a natural-bristle paintbrush. As the glaze begins to dry, it can be softened further by brushing the surface with a dry natural-bristle paintbrush. Complete one wall before moving on to the next or before stopping. Store any remaining glaze in a reclosable container between painting sessions.

The color-washing glaze can be either lighter or darker than the base coat. For best results, use two colors that are closely related or consider using a neutral color like beige or white for either the base coat or the glaze. Because the glaze is messy to work with, cover the floor and furniture with drop cloths and apply painter's tape along the ceiling and moldings.

COLOR-WASHING GLAZE

Mix together the following ingredients:

One part flat latex paint.

One part latex paint conditioner.

Two parts water.

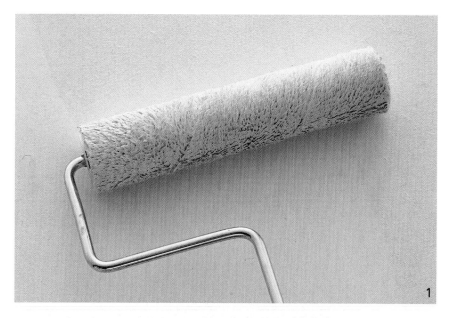

How to color wash walls

MATERIALS

- Low-luster latex enamel paint, for base coat.
- Flat latex paint, for color-washing glaze.
- Latex paint conditioner, for color-washing glaze.
- Paint roller.
- Two 3" to 4" (7.5 to 10 cm) natural-bristle paintbrushes for each person.
- Drop cloths; painter's tape.

1. Prepare the surface (page 13). Apply a base coat of low-luster latex enamel paint in the desired color, using a paint roller. Allow to dry.

2. Mix the color-washing glaze (page 55). Dip paintbrush into the glaze; remove excess glaze against rim of the container. Apply the glaze to wall in cross-hatching manner, beginning in one corner. The more you brush over the surface, the softer the appearance.

3. Brush over the surface, if desired, using a dry natural-bristle paintbrush, to soften the look. Wipe excess glaze from the brush as necessary.

A

B

C

COLOR EFFECTS

Select colors for the base coat and the glaze that are closely related, or use at least one neutral color. A darker glaze over a lighter base coat gives a mottled effect. A lighter glaze over a darker base coat gives a chalky or watercolored effect.

Apply a darker top coat, such as a medium turquoise, over a lighter base coat, such as white (A).

Apply a lighter top coat, such as white, over a darker base coat, such as coral (B).

Apply two shades of a color, such as a medium blue top coat over a light blue base coat (C).

Color-washed Finish for Wood

A subtle wash of color gives an appealing finish to wooden cabinets and accessories. This finish works for all decorating styles, from contemporary to country.

For color washing, a flat latex or acrylic paint is diluted with water. Applied over unfinished or stained wood, the color wash allows the natural wood tone and grain to show through. The lighter the original surface, the lighter the finished effect. To lighten a dark surface, first apply a white color wash, followed by a color wash in the desired finish color.

If you are applying a color wash to a varnished surface, remove any grease or dirt by washing the surface. It is important to roughen the varnish by sanding it, so the wood will accept the color-wash paint.

BELOW: COLOR-WASHED STRIPES have been applied to a wooden charger for a cheerful country accent.

How to apply a color-washed finish

MATERIALS

- Flat latex paint.
- Matte or low-gloss clear acrylic sealer or finish.
- Paintbrush.
- 220-grit sandpaper.
- Tack cloth.

1. Prepare wood surface by cleaning and sanding it; if surface is varnished, roughen it with sandpaper. Wipe with damp cloth.

2. Mix one part flat latex paint to four parts water. Apply to wood surface, brushing in direction of wood grain and working in an area no larger than 1 sq. yd. (0.95 sq. m) at a time. Allow to dry for 5 to 10 minutes.

3. Wipe surface with clean, lint-free cloth to partially remove paint, until desired effect is achieved. If the color is too light, repeat the process. Allow to dry. Lightly sand surface with 220-grit sandpaper to soften the look; wipe with damp cloth.

4. Apply one to two coats of clear acrylic sealer or finish, sanding lightly between coats.

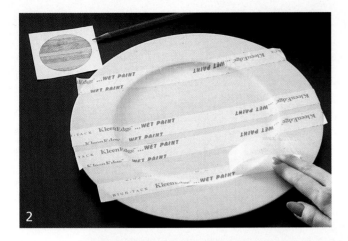

How to apply color-washed stripes

MATERIALS

- ◆ Craft acrylic paints in desired colors.
- ◆ 100-grit, 150-grit, and 220-grit sandpaper.
- ◆ Damp cloth.
- ◆ Painter's masking tape.
- ◆ Sponge applicator.
- ◆ Clear finish or aerosol clear acrylic sealer.

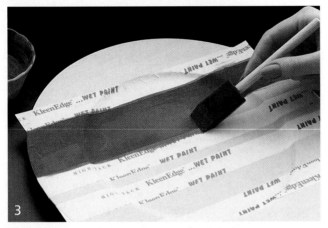

1. Sand the charger in the direction of the wood grain, using 150-grit sandpaper, then 220-grit sandpaper. Remove any grit, using a damp cloth.

2. Determine the desired color and width of each stripe in the charger, repeating colors as desired. Using painter's masking tape, mask off each side of stripes for the first paint color.

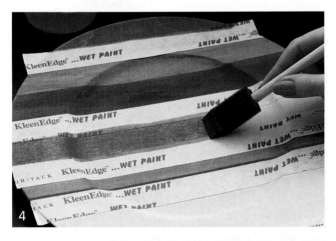

3. Dilute the paints, one part paint to two parts water. Apply the first paint color lightly to the masked stripes, using a sponge applicator; use paint sparingly. Allow to dry; remove tape.

4. Repeat steps 2 and 3 for each remaining paint color, allowing the paint to dry between colors.

5. Sand painted charger in the direction of wood grain, using 100-grit sandpaper, to give a worn appearance to the surface, especially sanding along outer and inner edges of the rim.

6. Apply a coat of clear finish or aerosol clear acrylic sealer to the charger. Apply additional coats as desired, sanding smooth between coats.

Faux Granite Finish

Duplicating the look of natural granite is very easy. By combining the techniques of sponge painting and specking, you can create a simulated granite that is so realistic, people may actually have to touch it before they realize it is a painted finish.

Natural granite is formed from molten stone and has a crystalline appearance. Granite colors from different regions of the world vary greatly, depending on how fast the molten lava cooled. The most common types of granite in America are composed of earth tones in burnt umber, raw umber, warm gray, black, and white. Some exotic granites consist of a rich combination of burgundy, purple, black, and gray; a fiery mix of copper, umber, black, and gray; the cool opalescence of metallic blue, black, pearl, and gray; or a warm combination or orange, red, and salmon.

OPPOSITE: METAL LAMP AND WOODEN FRAME are finished in two coordinating colors of granite.

COLOR EFFECTS

Granite colors vary from one part of the world to another. Use the color combinations below to simulate some of the natural granites that exist.

Apply a black base coat. Use sea sponge to apply paints in medium gray, light gray, and metallic silver. Speck with more light gray paint (A).

Apply a dark ivory base coat. Use a sea sponge to apply paints in brown, medium gray, dark gray, and black. Speck with more black paint (B).

Apply a medium gray base coat. Use sea sponge to apply dark gray, black, and metallic copper. Speck with more black paint (C).

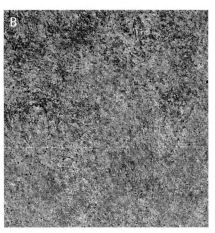
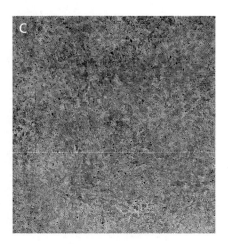

How to apply a faux granite finish

MATERIALS

- Flat latex or craft acrylic paint, for base coat.
- Flat latex or craft acrylic paint in desired colors, for sponging and specking; metallic paint may be used for one of the colors.
- Natural sea sponge.
- Fine-bristle scrub brush or toothbrush.
- Matte aerosol clear acrylic sealer or matte clear finish.

1. Prepare surface (page 13). Apply a base coat of flat latex or craft acrylic paint in white, gray, or black.

2. Dilute one paint color for sponging, one part paint to one part water, or to the consistency of ink; it may not be necessary to dilute metallic paint. Apply paint to surface in an up-and-down motion, using sea sponge.

3. Blot paint evenly with a clean, dampened sea sponge, immediately after applying it. This mottles the paint, blends it slightly with background color, and increases transparency. If the effect is not pleasing, wipe it off with a damp cloth before it dries.

4. Repeat steps 2 and 3 for remaining colors of paint for sponging, allowing each color to dry before the next color is applied. Allow some of the base coat to show through the other layers to create depth.

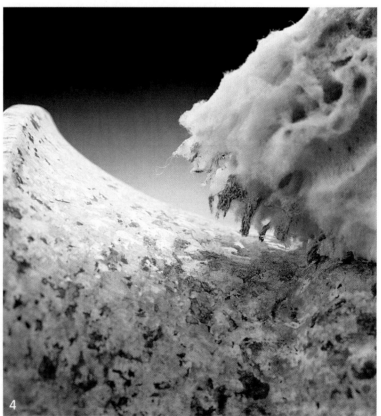

5. Apply diluted white, gray, or black paint to surface, using the specking technique, below. Speck the surface evenly in a light or moderate application.

6. Apply a matte aerosol clear acrylic sealer or clear finish to add sheen and depth and increase durability.

How to add specking

1. Dilute the paint for specking with water as in step 2, opposite. Test the paint consistency and technique by specking on cardboard before specking the actual project. Dip the bristles of a fine-bristle scrub brush or a toothbrush into the paint mixture. Dab once on a dry paper towel, to remove excess moisture and prevent drips.

2. Hold the brush next to surface; run craft stick or finger along bristles, causing specks of paint to spatter onto surface. Experiment with how fast you move the craft stick and how far away you hold the brush. Too much paint on the brush may cause paint to drip or run.

Faux Unpolished Stone Finish

Unpolished stone, in many colors and textures, is used extensively by the building industry, both in its natural state and cut into stone blocks. Just as genuine unpolished stones vary in surface textures, different faux painting techniques can be used to create faux unpolished stone finishes that are very different from each other. The painting technique of stippling results in a relatively smooth textured finish with blended colors. A stippler is repeatedly pounced over the surface, blending glazes and creating a fine-grained texture. Another method, using newspaper, results in an unpolished stone finish with depth, color variation, and rough visual texture.

Flat earth-tone glazes are used in all methods to create faux finishes that mimic real unpolished stones. Use the glazes suggested here, or select other earth-tone colors, as desired. For a faux finish resembling stone block, mask off grout lines and apply the finish to each stone individually. This allows you to vary the depth of color in adjacent stones. If applying the finish to a large, undivided surface, work in smaller areas at a time, leaving a wet edge. When dry, the painted stone may be left unsealed, or sealed with a matte finish.

MATERIALS

- ◆ White low-luster latex enamel paint, for base coat; sponge applicator or paintbrush, for smaller surface; sponge or low-napped roller, for larger surface.
- ◆ Flat paint glazes (page 14) in a variety of earth-tone colors, black, and white.
- ◆ Stippler (page 10), for stippling method.
- ◆ Newspaper, for newspaper method.
- ◆ White wash; earth-tone wash (page 14); cheesecloth.
- ◆ Matte aerosol clear acrylic sealer or matte clear finish, optional.

How to apply a faux unpolished stone finish using the stippling method

1. Prepare the surface (page 13). Apply base coat of white low-luster latex enamel to the surface, using applicator suitable to surface size. Allow to dry. Mask off grout lines, if desired.

2. Apply flat earth-tone glaze in random strokes, using sponge applicator or paintbrush; cover about half the surface. Repeat with another color glaze in remaining areas; leave some small areas of base coat unglazed.

3. Stipple over surface, using stippler; blend colors as desired, leaving some areas quite dark and others very light where base coat shows through. Add white and black glazes, if desired; add earth-tone glazes as necessary. Stipple to blend. Allow to dry.

4. Apply white wash to the entire surface. Dab with wadded cheesecloth to soften. Allow to dry. Apply matte clear finish or matte aerosol clear acrylic sealer, if desired.

How to apply a faux unpolished stone finish using the newspaper method

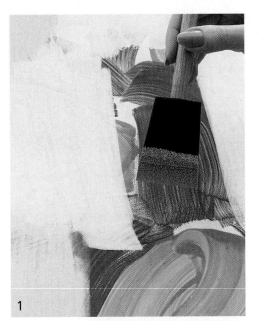

1. Follow steps 1 and 2, opposite. Apply white wash in areas desired; apply earth-tone wash in areas desired.

2. Fold a sheet of newspaper to several layers. Lay it flat over one area of surface and press into the glaze. Lift, removing some glaze. Repeat in other areas, turning same newspaper in different directions to blend colors roughly.

3. Add more color to an area by spreading glaze on newspaper and laying it flat on surface. Repeat as necessary until desired effect is achieved. Leave some dark accent areas in finish; also leave an occasional light spot. Use same newpaper throughout. Allow to dry.

4. Apply white wash to entire surface. Dab with a wadded cheesecloth to soften. Allow to dry. Apply matte clear finish or matte aerosol clear acrylic sealer, if desired.

Faux Tigereye Finish

Tigereye is a semiprecious stone often used in jewelry or small ornamental pieces. This dark, glassy stone is characterized by undulating narrow bands of gold that have a changeable luster, like the eye of a cat.

The gold bands of a faux tigereye finish are created by first covering the surface with gold metallic paint, or, for a rich, luminous look, gold leaf. A raw umber gloss glaze is applied over the gold surface and combed, using the notched edge of an eraser, to reveal irregular bands of gold. After drying, a final wash (page 14) is drawn across the bands in the opposite direction, forming shadowy streaks that give the tigereye its undulating quality. A high-gloss finish is an essential last step, giving the tigereye finish a glassy brilliance.

Tigereye finish is appropriate for small, flat surfaces, such as a wooden box lid or picture frame. For an inlaid effect, a border of tigereye finish can be applied around the outer edge of a small table or tray.

MATERIALS

- Acrylic or latex paint in metallic gold color, for base coat; sponge applicator.
- Soft artist's eraser; mat knife.
- Raw umber gloss glaze; sponge applicator or paintbrush; newspaper.
- Cheesecloth.
- Raw umber wash.
- High-gloss clear finish or high-gloss aerosol clear acrylic sealer.

How to apply a faux tigereye finish

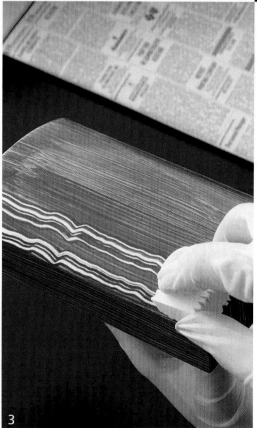

1. Prepare the surface (page 13). Apply base coat of gold metallic paint, or apply gold leaf and sealer. Notch edges of eraser in irregular pattern, using mat knife. Test notch patterns by pulling eraser edges through thin glaze spread on tagboard scrap. Each notched edge should leave clean, irregularly spaced stripes of varying widths from fine lines to 1/4" (6 mm) wide. Adjust the notches, if necessary.

2. Apply raw umber gloss glaze to surface, using sponge applicator or paintbrush; draw brush across surface in parallel lines.

3. Comb through glaze in direction of brush strokes, using notched edge of eraser. Start at outer edge of surface; move eraser slowly from top to bottom in continuous motion, creating gold bands with irregular small waves, dips, and peaks. Wipe excess glaze from eraser onto newspaper.

4. Comb through glaze next to previous bands, using another notched edge of eraser; vaguely follow pattern of previous bands. Wipe excess glaze from eraser. Repeat until entire surface has been combed, varying width of bands and spaces between them.

5. Dab surface with wadded cheesecloth, slightly softening gold bands. Allow to dry thoroughly.

6. Apply wash to the surface with sponge applicator, stroking in the opposite direction of gold bands and making wash more visible in some areas than others; allow hand to tremble, creating shadowy streaks. Allow to dry thoroughly.

7. Apply several thin coats of high-gloss clear finish or high-gloss aerosol clear acrylic sealer, allowing the surface to dry between coats.

Faux Malachite Finish

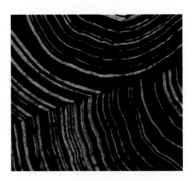

The distinctive banding pattern and vibrant green color of malachite make this semiprecious stone instantly recognizable. A cross-section of malachite reveals egg-shaped nodules surrounded by multiple bands, varying in width and intensity, that seem to echo from the nodules like ripples of water. The bands of malachite will vary from nearly straight to sharply curved. Genuine malachite in solid form is used in jewelry and carved objects, while thin slices of the stone are often inlaid in mosaic fashion on tabletops or other flat surfaces.

The painting technique used to simulate malachite is combing, using an irregularly notched edge of an artist's eraser. Malachite is usually depicted as pieced geometric sections on a small, flat surface, with the banding direction changing at each adjoining line. Some sections may show a partial nodule, created by combing in a tight, oval shape, with surrounding bands that echo from the nodule. Other sections may contain only bands with varying degrees of curve. The bands often have a characteristic V-formation, created by combing in an arc, hesitating, and then changing direction into a new arc. A final high-gloss finish gives faux malachite its characteristic depth and luster. It is helpful to sketch the layout of the sections and the pattern of banding in each section before beginning to paint. Also, practice the combing method to achieve the look of genuine malachite.

MATERIALS

- Paper and pencil, for sketching design.
- White low-luster latex enamel paint, for base coat; sponge applicator or paint brush.
- Bright green or blue-green latex or craft acrylic paint, acrylic urethane, for ure thane glaze.
- Painter's masking tape.
- Very dark hunter or forest green gloss glaze (page 14).

- Sponge applicator or paintbrush, for applying glazes.
- Soft artist's eraser; mat knife or razor blade.
- Newspaper.
- Cheesecloth.
- Denatured alcohol; round artist's brush.
- High-gloss aerosol clear acrylic sealer or high-gloss clear finish.

URETHANE GLAZE

Mix together the following ingredients:

One part bright green or blue-green latex paint or craft acrylic paint.

One part acrylic urethane.

One part water.

Making a sketch of the design

1. Outline design area to scale on piece of paper. Divide design area into sections, avoiding acute and square angles whenever possible. Sketch banding pattern in each section, including partial nodules in some sections; vary banding direction and degree of curve in adjoining sections.

How to apply a faux malachite finish

1. Prepare surface (page 13). Apply base coat of white low-luster latex enamel to surface, using sponge applicator. Allow to dry. Mix urethane glaze (page 31); apply to entire design area, using sponge applicator or paintbrush. Brush entire area first in one direction and then in opposite direction, leveling glaze. Allow to dry thoroughly. Divide design area into sections with light pencil lines, following sketch. Mask off first section to be glazed. Notch eraser edges as in step 1 on page 28.

2. Apply very dark green gloss glaze to first design section, using sponge applicator or paintbrush. Comb notched eraser edge through glaze, following sketched banding pattern, beginning and ending combing motion just beyond design area. If pattern contains nodule, comb it first. Allow hand to waver occasionally. Wipe excess glaze from eraser onto newspaper.

3. Comb through glaze next to previous bands, using another notched edge of eraser; follow pattern of previous bands, gradually widening arc on curved banding patterns. Repeat until section is completely combed. Remove tape.

4. Mask off next section that does not adjoin previously glazed section. Apply glaze; comb, following sketch. Remove tape. Repeat for remaining sections that do not adjoin. Allow to dry.

5. Mask off a section that adjoins a previously glazed section; position tape edge so hairline of glazed section is exposed. Apply glaze; comb, following sketch. Remove tape. Repeat for remaining unglazed sections until design is complete. Allow to dry.

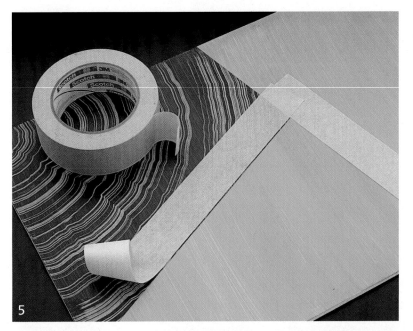

6. Dilute dark green glaze with water to consistency of wash (page 14). Apply over entire design; dab with wadded cheesecloth to soften.

7. Spatter immediately with denatured alcohol, using round paintbrush in random, sparse application. Allow to dry thoroughly.

8. Apply several thin coats of high-gloss aerosol clear acrylic sealer or high-gloss clear finish, allowing the surface to dry between coats.

Faux Lapis Finish

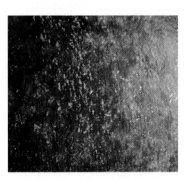

Lapis is a deep blue semiprecious stone flecked with lustrous, golden mineral deposits. The blue color builds and recedes in drifts, in spots revealing pale gray tones. Because of its scarcity, it is generally used in fine jewelry or small, ornate accessories.

Faux lapis is applied, using a stippling technique. Two different deep blue paint glazes are stippled onto the surface in diagonal drifts, sometimes blending with each other and at other times remaining separate, thus creating the characteristic depth of color. Droplets of denatured alcohol, sprinkled over the wet glaze, cause amorphous rings in the glaze. Gold powder is sprinkled over the wet glaze and gently pressed into the surface to resemble mineral deposits. After drying, a high-gloss aerosol acrylic sealer is applied for a glassy appearance.

For a realistic appearance, faux lapis can be applied to any small paintable surface, such as a ceramic vase. It can also be applied as inlaid sections on a flat surface.

When using metallic powders, avoid any drafts that may blow the powder around and wear a protective mask to prevent inhaling the fine particles.

MATERIALS

- Light gray low-luster latex enamel paint, for base coat; sponge applicator or paintbrush.
- Prussian blue gloss glaze (page 14).
- Cobalt blue gloss glaze (page 14).
- Stippler (page 10), in size suitable to project.
- Denatured alcohol; round artist's paintbrush.
- Cheesecloth.
- Gold powder; protective mask.
- High-gloss aerosol clear acrylic sealer.

How to apply a faux lapis finish

1. Prepare surface (page 13). Apply base coat of light gray low-luster latex enamel to surface, using sponge applicator or paintbrush. Allow to dry. Apply Prussian blue gloss glaze in random strokes, using sponge applicator or paintbrush; cover about half the surface. Repeat with cobalt blue gloss glaze in remaining areas; leave some small areas of base coat unglazed.

2. Stipple over entire area, blending colors slightly and leaving lighter small areas where base coat shows through.

3. Spatter droplets of denatured alcohol over wet glaze, using round artist's brush; apply droplets in diagonal drifts. Allow alcohol to react in glaze.

4. Dab some alcohol droplets with wadded cheesecloth to soften; leave other droplets undisturbed. Apply more Prussian blue glaze onto surface in diagonal drifts; repeat, using cobalt blue glaze. Stipple, blending colors slightly.

5. Repeat steps 3 and 4. Load small amount of gold metallic powder on dry round artist's brush. Hold brush about 12" (30.5 cm) above surface; tap the brush gently, allowing the powder to fall onto darker areas of the surface in small concentrations.

6. Press gold powder gently into the surface with wadded cheesecloth.

7. Repeat steps 5 and 6 as desired. Apply more Prussian blue glaze in some areas, deepening color; soften with cheesecloth. Repeat step 3 over fresh glaze. Allow entire surface to dry thoroughly. Apply several thin coats of high-gloss aerosol clear acrylic sealer, allowing surface to dry between coats.

FAUX MARBLE FINISHES

Faux Onyx Finish

Onyx is a black semiprecious mineral with wispy bands of white that resemble the veins found in many marbles. It has long been used for small carvings or accessories, accentuating the high contrast between the black background and white bands.

To create the white bands in a faux onyx finish, acrylic extender and acrylic thickener are applied alongside white paint, using a turkey feather. This results in wispy bands that fluctuate from opaque to translucent. A high-gloss finish gives the faux onyx a glassy, polished look.

MATERIALS

- Black craft acrylic or flat latex paint, for base coat.
- White craft acrylic paint.
- Acrylic paint thickener.
- Acrylic paint extender.
- Natural sea sponge.
- Two turkey or pheasant feathers.
- Disposable plate.
- High-gloss aerosol clear acrylic sealer.

How to apply a faux onyx finish

1. Prepare surface (page 13). Apply a base coat of black craft acrylic or flat latex paint. Allow to dry.

2. Apply a long pool of white paint onto a disposable plate. Apply pool of thickener on one side of white paint and extender on the other.

3. Run edge of feather through pools, picking up some thickener, paint, and extender on feather; cover the entire length of feather. Blot excess onto paper towel.

4. Zigzag the feather across base coat in 3" to 4" (7.5 to 10 cm) irregular diagonal bands, with some of the bands meeting or intersecting. Work on only two or three bands at a time, because paint dries quickly.

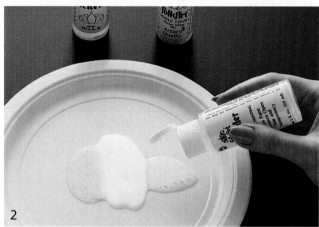

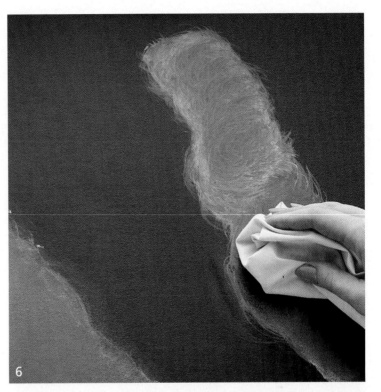

5. Smear the bands of white in a circular motion, using moist sea sponge, for the look of softened light clouds.

6. Rub the bands lightly while still wet, using a dry rag, to give them the appearance of dust on a chalkboard; do not rub over the black base coat. Reapply white paint if too much is rubbed away. If surface dries too quickly, apply water, then rub with rag to soften. Allow to dry.

7. Run edge of the feather through pools of thickener, paint, and extender; blot on paper towel. Place tip of feather onto surface; drag the feather along, fidgeting it and turning it slightly in your hand to create veins. Outline chalky bands with veins; apply more veins in a diagonal direction, crisscrossing them as desired. The thickener and extender vary the veins so some areas are opaque and some are translucent. Allow the paint to dry. Apply several coats of high-gloss aerosol clear acrylic sealer.

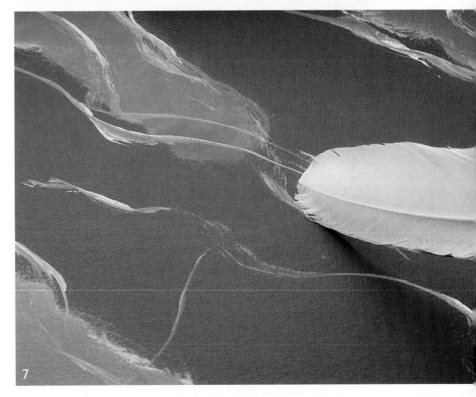

Faux Serpentine Finish

Serpentine is the general name given to a variety of green marbles that contain deposits of the mineral, serpentine. The different varieties vary in visual texture and color tone, often with traces of black and white. Some serpentines may be characterized by a network of fine veining, while others contain little or no veining. As with other marbles, the serpentines have various architectural uses, including floors, walls, and pillars.

Just as genuine marble is cut into workable pieces for installation, a faux serpentine finish applied to a large surface is more realistic if applied in sections with narrow grout lines. By masking off alternate sections, the finish can be applied to half the project, following steps 1 to 9. When the first half has been allowed to dry completely, the completed sections can be masked off, and the finish can be applied to the remaining sections. A high-gloss finish is then applied to the entire surface, giving the faux finish the lustrous appearance of genuine marble.

MATERIALS

- Medium green low-luster latex enamel paint, for base coat; sponge applicator or paintbrush, for small surface, or low-napped roller, for larger surface.
- Black gloss glaze (page 14).
- Green gloss glaze (page 14), in darker shade than base coat
- White gloss glaze (page 14).
- Newspaper, cheesecloth, stippler, for applying and working glaze.
- Spray bottle; water.
- Turkey feather, for veining.
- High-gloss clear finish or high-gloss aerosol clear acrylic sealer.

How to apply a faux serpentine finish

1. Prepare surface (page 13). Apply base coat of medium green low-luster latex enamel to surface, using applicator suitable to surface size. Apply black, green and white gloss glazes separately in random, broad, diagonal strokes, using sponge applicator or paintbrush; cover most of surface, allowing small patches of base coat to show through.

2. Stipple the glazes in adjoining areas to blend slightly, pouncing stippler rapidly over the surface.

3. Fold a sheet of newspaper to several layers; lay flat over an area of surface, in the same diagonal direction as original strokes. Press newspaper into glaze; lift, removing some of glaze.

4. Repeat step 3 over entire surface, using same newspaper; turn paper in opposite direction occasionally. Add glazes as desired to develop color. Dab areas of high contrast with wadded cheesecloth, to soften. Mist surface with water, if necessary, to keep glazes workable.

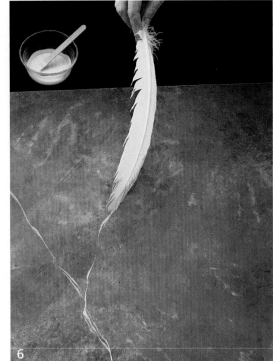

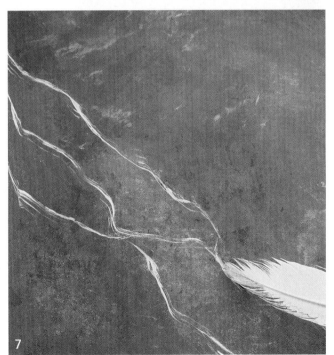

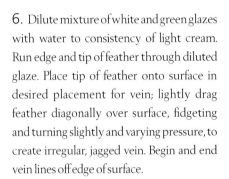

5. Brush black glaze onto newspaper and touch to surface diagonally in scattered areas, adding drama and depth. Soften with cheesecloth, if necessary. Repeat, using white glaze in small, lighter areas.

6. Dilute mixture of white and green glazes with water to consistency of light cream. Run edge and tip of feather through diluted glaze. Place tip of feather onto surface in desired placement for vein; lightly drag feather diagonally over surface, fidgeting and turning slightly and varying pressure, to create irregular, jagged vein. Begin and end vein lines off edge of surface.

7. Repeat step 6 as desired to build veining pattern; connect adjacent vein lines occasionally, creating narrow, oblong, irregular shapes. Dab veins lightly with wadded cheesecloth to soften, if necessary. Allow surface to dry.

8. Dilute glazes to consistency of wash (page 14); apply randomly to surface. Dab with wadded cheesecloth to soften. Allow to dry. Apply several thin coats of high-gloss clear finish or high-gloss aerosol clear acrylic sealer, allowing surface to dry between coats.

GOLD VEINING GLAZE

Mix together the following ingredients:

One part gold metallic craft acrylic paint.

One part acrylic urethane.

One part water.

Faux Portoro Finish

Portoro, also known as black and gold marble, has been used for centuries in architecture and for smaller-scale decorative work. It is characterized by networks of fibrous veining, usually 1" to 3" (2.5 to 7.5 cm) wide and running in very linear patterns through wide expanses of black marble. The veining networks are often gold in color, though the color can be more off-white or beige. Distinctive white secondary veins intersect the networks at opposing angles, threading over or under the veining in staggered lines.

Select faux Portoro for a dramatic finish on a bathroom wall or fireplace surround. On a smaller scale, paint a faux Portoro finish on a table base or pedestal. Apply the finish with the veining networks running horizontally or vertically. If possible, turn the work so that you are working vertically from top to bottom, since the veining brush will be held at right angles to the veining network. Start and end veining networks off the surface, implying visually that they continued beyond the cut marble.

OPPOSITE: THE FAUX PORTORO FINISH makes it look as though this pedestal has been carved from solid marble. A high-gloss finish makes the illusion even more believable.

MATERIALS

- Black low-luster latex enamel paint, for base coat; sponge applicator or paintbrush, for small surface area, or roller, for larger area.
- Gold metallic acrylic paint, acrylic urethane, for gold veining glaze.
- Round artist's brush.

- White gloss glaze (page 14).
- Black wash (page 14).
- Cheesecloth.
- High-gloss clear finish or high-gloss aerosol clear acrylic sealer.

How to apply a faux Portoro finish

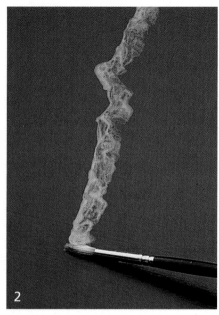

1. Prepare surface (page 13). Apply base coat of black low-luster latex enamel to surface, using applicator suitable to surface size. Allow to dry.

2. Mix gold veining glaze (page 48). Dip round artist's brush into water, then into glaze. Hold the brush sideways at upper edge of surface, at right angle to line of veining network; hold brush between thumb and fingers near end of handle, with thumb on top. Pull brush toward lower edge, rolling brush handle back and forth and fidgeting to create irregular, jagged veining line.

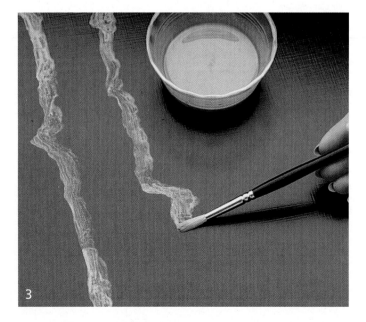

3. Repeat step 2 in second vein alongside first vein; add third vein as desired.

4. Dip brush into water, then into glaze. Paint thin, fidgety lines connecting adjacent veins, using the tip of the brush; also, form small nodules here and there along one side of each main vein by connecting jagged points.

5. Allow gold veining networks to dry. Dip brush into water, then into white glaze. Paint a few thin, fidgety lines at opposing angles to veining networks; avoid right angles. Cross directly over the top of some veining networks; on others break the white line as it passes behind gold veins. Allow to dry.

6. Apply black wash to entire surface. Dab with wadded cheesecloth to soften. Allow to dry.

7. Apply several thin coats of high-gloss clear finish or high-gloss aerosol clear acrylic sealer, allowing surface to dry between coats.

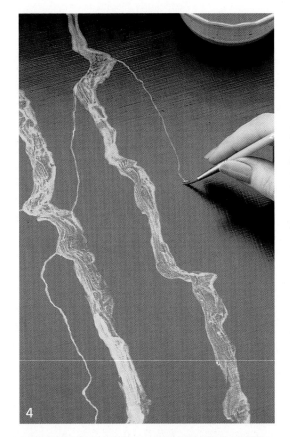

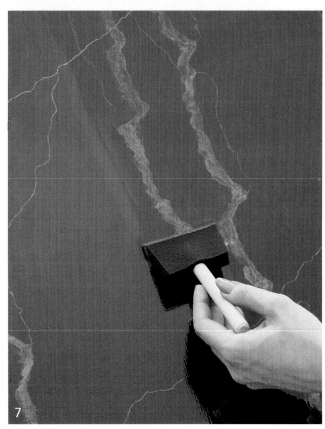

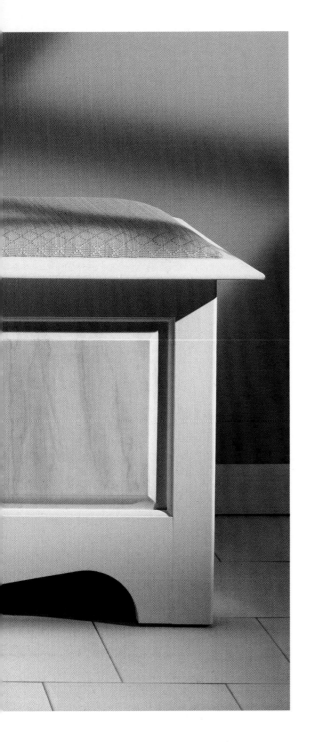

Faux Norwegian Rose Finish

Norwegian rose is a white marble with patches of pink and green mineral deposits that give the marble its striking contrast of colors. Patchy drifts of dusty pink color fade into hues of taupe and tan, surrounded by a gray-green veining structure.

The decorative uses for a faux Norwegian rose marble finish include floor or wall tiles, pillars, accessories, and tabletops. The marble pattern, determined by the direction of the veining structure, can be set up vertically, horizontally, or at an angle, depending on the desired effect.

MATERIALS

- White low-luster latex enamel paint, for base coat; sponge applicator or paintbrush, for small surface, or low-napped roller, for larger surface.
- White gloss glaze (page 14).
- Pink gloss glaze (page 14).
- Tan gloss glaze (page 14).
- Raw umber gloss glaze (page 14).
- Sponge applicator, cheesecloth, feather, blending brush, for applying and working glazes.
- White wash (page 14).
- High-gloss clear finish or high-gloss aerosol clear acrylic sealer.

How to apply a faux Norwegian rose finish

1

2

3

4

1. Prepare surface (page 13). Apply base coat of white low-luster latex enamel to surface, using applicator suitable to surface size. Apply pink gloss glaze to surface in a few random oval patches, angling ovals in desired direction of marble pattern.

2. Apply narrow patches of tan gloss glaze along the sides of some pink patches, running tan areas together. Avoid any regular pattern or balanced placement. Apply white gloss glaze in remaining areas. Dab with wadded cheesecloth to soften and blend adjoining colors.

3. Whisk over the surface in desired direction of the marble pattern, using blending brush (page 10) to soften and elongate patches of color. Whisk occasionally in the direction perpendicular to pattern to widen patches slightly.

4. Apply more glaze, dab with cheesecloth, and whisk as needed to achieve the desired look. Repeat for all areas of surface.

5. Run edge and tip of feather through the raw umber glaze; drag the feather over the surface, roughly outlining patches of color. Connect adjacent vein lines, creating narrow, oblong, irregular shapes.

6. Dab veins lightly with wadded cheesecloth to soften. Whisk with blending brush to elongate and blur vein lines. Allow to dry.

7. Apply white wash to the surface; dab with wadded cheesecloth to soften. Whisk with blending brush. Allow to dry. Apply several thin coats of high-gloss clear finish or high-gloss aerosol clear acrylic sealer, allowing the surface to dry between coats.

Faux Travertine Finish

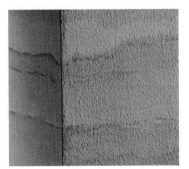

Travertine is a type of limestone used extensively in architecture, especially for large surfaces, such as floors and walls. It is formed when water from underground springs deposits layer upon layer of minerals in faulted horizontal bands. Throughout the layers of mineral deposits, small pits are created as the water evaporates. These open pits are very evident in unpolished travertine, the form used most often. For some uses of travertine, the surface pits are filled and the stone is polished. Because of its very linear structure, travertine can be used vertically, horizontally, or diagonally for different effects.

For a faux travertine finish, flat earth-tone glazes are applied in narrow, blended bands over a white base coat. Denatured alcohol is applied to the wet glaze, mottling the bands with swirls and voids that resemble the mineral deposits and pits in the stone. These mottled bands are separated by wide, pale bands that are very lightly streaked. When applying the finish to a large, unbroken surface, such as a wall or tabletop, apply all mottled bands first. Repeat steps 2 through 5 for each mottled band, working in rough 24" (61 cm) lengths and keeping a wet edge until the entire band is complete. When all mottled bands are dry, apply thinned glaze, as in steps 7 and 8. Then apply all separating layers (steps 9 and 10). When all layers have been completed, the final wash and optional matte finish can be applied to the entire surface. The finish may also be applied in sections, resembling stone blocks, allowing you to work on one block at a time.

How to apply a faux travertine finish

MATERIALS

- White low-luster latex enamel paint, for base coat; sponge applicator, paintbrush, or roller.
- Flat raw sienna glaze (page 14).
- Flat raw umber glaze (page 14).
- Flat white glaze (page 14).
- Stippler.
- Spray bottle with water.
- Denatured alcohol; round artist's paintbrush.
- Cheesecloth.
- Blending brush or softener.
- Ivory wash (page 14).
- Matte clear finish or matte aerosol clear acrylic sealer, optional.

1. Prepare surface (page 13). Apply base coat of white low-luster latex enamel to surface, using applicator suitable to surface size. Allow to dry.

2. Apply narrow bands of flat raw sienna glaze, flat raw umber glaze, and flat white glaze next to each other on surface, breaking and staggering bands randomly.

3

4

3 Stipple bands of glaze in adjoining areas, blending colors slightly. Mist with water to keep surface moist.

4. Dip round artist's paintbrush into denatured alcohol; touch tip of brush into wet glaze, applying small amounts of alcohol throughout stippled band. Reload brush as needed.

5. Roll brush through band, redistributing alcohol. Allow alcohol to react with glaze, creating swirls and voids throughout the band. Dab with cheesecloth as needed, to soften effect.

Continued

5

How to apply a faux travertine finish

(CONTINUED)

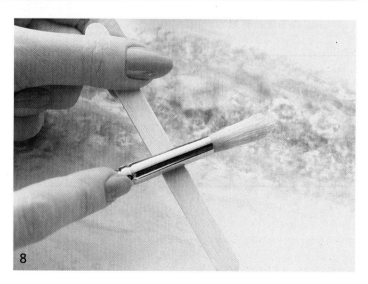

6. Repeat steps 2 through 5 for each mottled band, allowing spaces for separating bands two to four times the width of mottled band. Allow mottled bands to dry.

7. Thin white glaze with water to consistency of light cream. Apply to mottled band, using sponge applicator or paintbrush; dab with wadded cheesecloth to soften.

8. Spatter denatured alcohol throughout band; stipple. Add more thinned glaze as desired; repeat alcohol application.

9. Repeat steps 7 and 8 for each mottled band. Sideload the brush with small amount of raw umber glaze; dip in thinned white glaze. Draw the brush through separating band several times, forming watery, pale streaks. Allow to dry slightly.

10. Brush over the slightly dry separating band with light strokes in opposite direction, using dry blending brush.

11. Repeat steps 9 and 10 for all separating bands. Allow the entire surface to dry thoroughly. Apply ivory wash, using sponge applicator or paintbrush; dab with wadded cheesecloth to soften. Allow to dry. Apply matte clear finish or matte aerosol clear acrylic sealer, if desired.

PAINTED FINISHES

Enamel Paint Finish

The timeless look of white painted cabinets is appropriate for any decorating style. With the use of good equipment and high-quality paint, you can achieve a professional-looking finish on most wood types, depending on the grain of the wood.

The enamel paint may be applied with a high-quality paintbrush. However, for best results when painting large areas like cabinet doors and drawer fronts, it is recommended that the paint be applied with a sprayer. The use of a sprayer prevents any brush strokes or ridges caused by a paintbrush, paint roller, or sponge applicator.

There are two main types of paint sprayers: airless and air. Although airless sprayers are known to clog and apply paint unevenly, air sprayers perform with excellent results.

The air sprayers are a commercial grade of sprayer referred to as LPHV, meaning low pressure and high volume. Available from rental stores, they apply paint in an even coat without clogging and with minimal overspray. They are easy to use, even for do-it-yourselfers. The width of the spray area and the amount of the paint that is released are adjustable. Because the operation instructions may vary somewhat from one brand to another, practice on a large sheet of cardboard until you are accustomed to using the sprayer and have the spray flow properly adjusted. After each use, clean the sprayer according to the manufacturer's instructions.

Use a high-gloss latex enamel paint for a durable, smooth finish. For a smooth application, dilute the paint with a latex paint conditioner, according to the manufacturer's instructions. The ratio of paint to conditioner varies, depending on whether a sprayer or paintbrush is used. Dilute only the amount of paint that you intend to use in a day, and use the same ratio each day. Before applying the paint, prepare the wood surface as on page 9.

How to apply an enamel paint finish

MATERIALS

- High-gloss latex enamel paint.
- Latex paint conditioner, such as Floetrol®.
- LPHV air paint sprayer, available from rental stores.
- High-quality synthetic paintbrush.
- 220-grit sandpaper.
- Tack cloth.

1. Unscrew the doorknobs and drawer pulls; remove cabinet doors and drawers. Prepare all wood surfaces (page 9). Mask off any surfaces that are not to be painted.

2. Fill air sprayer according to manufacturer's instructions. Practice painting on large sheet of cardboard, adjusting spray flow for a smooth, light application of paint with no runs.

3. Spray the cabinet doors and drawer fronts in a clean, well-ventilated area, applying light coat of paint. Clean the sprayer. Allow paint to dry for 8 hours.

4. Paint cabinet interiors and edges of cabinets, using paintbrush; allow to dry for 8 hours. Apply additional coats of paint as necessary.

5. Repeat step 3 to apply at least three light coats of paint, allowing each coat to dry for 8 hours. Paint back sides of the doors after the door fronts are thoroughly dry, using a sprayer or paintbrush.

6. Secure the doorknobs and drawer pulls when the paint is thoroughly dry. Hang cabinet doors.

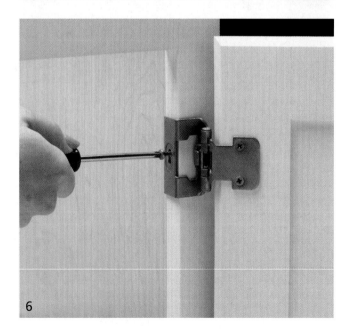

Crackled Finish

This paint finish transforms wooden kitchen cabinets, furniture, and accessories into pieces with the timeworn look of antiques. Crackling, a technique developed in response to the increasing appeal of aged furnishings, uses contemporary products to imitate the effects of aging and weathering on paint. A crackled finish can be applied to unfinished wood or previously varnished or painted wood.

A base color of paint is applied to a prepared wood surface, followed first by a crackle medium, then by a top coat of paint in a second color. Almost instantly, the crackle medium causes the top coat of paint to crackle randomly, revealing the base color. To give an even more aged appearance, artist's oil paints can be rubbed randomly onto the crackled surface. A clear acrylic finish is applied as a final coat for durability.

Acrylic and latex paints can be successfully crackled; be consistent in using either acrylic or latex paint for the base coat and the top coat. Because the composition of paints varies from brand to brand, some paints may not crackle as desired. Test the products on a scrap of lumber before working on the actual project, varying the length of time the crackle medium sets before the top coat of paint is applied. The thickness of the top coat can also change the look of the crackling. Because the crackle medium may tend to run, apply it horizontally whenever possible.

For a prominent crackling effect, select light and dark contrasting paint colors. For the optional artist's oil paints, select a color similar to the base coat to mix with a gray or brown. This gives a muted effect that is compatible with the color of the crackling.

How to apply a crackled finish

MATERIALS

- Paint in two colors for base coat and top coat; paintbrush.
- Crackle medium, such as Quick-Crackle™.
- Artist's oil paints in two colors, selected as described on page 21, optional.
- 220-grit sandpaper
- Clear acrylic finish.

1. Prepare wood surface (page 9). Apply a base coat of paint in desired color to the wood surface. Allow to dry.

2. Apply even, light coat of crackle medium over the base coat. Allow to set for length of time specified by the manufacturer or according to your own test results for desired crackling effect. For a large project, such as a cabinet, work on a limited area at a time, so you do not exceed setting time.

3. Apply paint in a contrasting color; paint will crackle soon after it is applied. Allow top coat to dry.

4. Give crackled finish a more aged appearance, if desired, by mixing two artist's oil paints together. Rub small amounts of mixed oil paint onto the crackled surface, following wood grain; reapply until the desired effect is achieved. If too much oil paint is applied to an area, remove excess by sanding lightly with 220-grit sandpaper; wipe sanded surface with tack cloth.

5. Apply one or two coats of clear acrylic finish, for added durability.

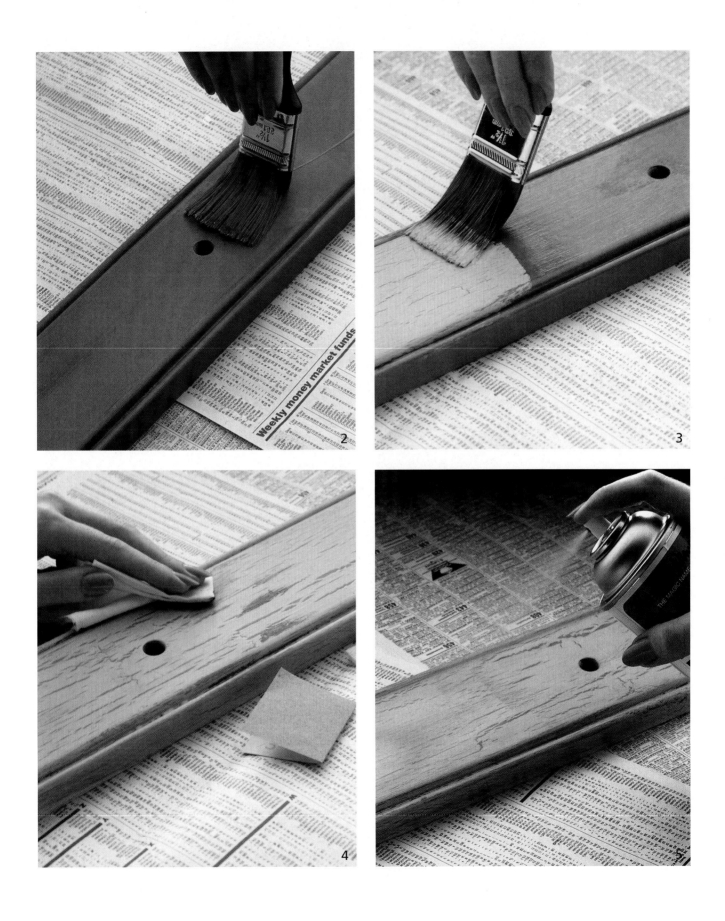

Faux Moiré

For the watermarked look of silk moiré fabric, use a process similar to the wood-graining technique of faux wood. The subtle tone-on-tone pattern can be created in any color for a coordinated decorating scheme. This finish is recommended for small areas, such as below a chair rail or within frame moldings.

A rocker tool designed for wood graining is used for this watermarked effect. A paint glaze (page 26) is applied over a base coat of paint, and the graining tool is pulled and rocked through the glaze to create impressions. Then a dry paintbrush is pulled across the markings to mimic the crosswise grain of moiré.

The glaze used for faux moiré contains more paint than most glazes, making it thicker and more opaque. In order to finish the graining before the glaze has dried, apply the glaze to a small area at a time. If faux moiré is used on the wall area below a chair rail or border, work from the chair rail to the baseboard in 12" (30.5 cm) sections, working quickly.

Moiré is simulated by using a darker shade for the base coat and a lighter glaze for the top coat. This gives the brighter sheen that is characteristic of moiré fabric.

How to apply a faux moiré paint finish

MATERIALS

- Low-luster latex enamel paint in darker shade, for base coat.

- Low-luster enamel paint in lighter shade, for glaze; or base-coat paint, lightened with white paint, may be used.

- Latex paint conditioner, such as Floetrol®.

- Wood-graining rocker.

- Paint roller or paintbrush, for applying the base coat and the glaze.

- Natural-bristle paintbrush, 2″ to 3″ (5 to 7.5 cm) wide, for dry brushing.

FAUX MOIRÉ GLAZE

Mix together the following ingredients:

Two parts semigloss latex enamel paint.

One part latex paint conditioner.

One part water.

1. Prepare surface and apply base coat of low-luster latex enamel. Allow to dry.

2. Mix glaze. Apply an even coat of glaze over a base coat to a small area at a time, rolling or brushing vertically.

3. Slide graining tool vertically through wet glaze, occasionally rocking it slowly back and forth, to create watermarked effect. Start at one corner, working in one continuous motion as you slide and rock the tool from one end to another. As you rock the tool, oval markings are created.

4. Repeat step 3 for subsequent rows; stagger the oval markings, and work quickly before glaze dries. Wipe the excess glaze from tool as necessary.

5. Pull dry brush horizontally across surface when glaze has partially dried, using a natural-bristle paintbrush; this mimics the crosswise grain of the moiré fabric. Wipe excess glaze from the brush as necessary. Allow paint to dry.

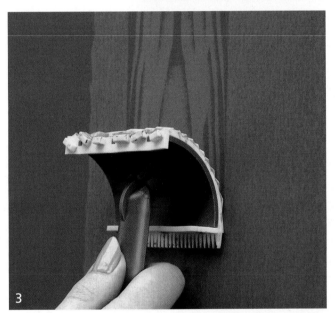

PAINTED
DESIGNS

Easy Freehand Designs

Simple designs are easy to paint freehand, even if you do not consider yourself an artist. Discover many possible designs by looking at fabrics, wallcoverings, and gift-wrapping papers. When painting repetitive designs, you can allow the designs to vary slightly to emphasize the handmade quality, rather than painstakingly try to paint identical designs. Add interest to the painted pieces by using different designs to highlight separate areas of a single item.

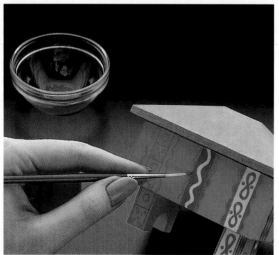

MARK simple freehand designs, using light pencil lines. Fill in the marked areas with paint, allowing the paint to dry between colors.

TRANSFER designs that are more intricate, using the methods on pages 23 to 27. Use appropriate artist's brush to fill in the design areas. When hand painting, you do not have to follow the marked design exactly.

Swirled Designs

Swirls of paint created with sweeping brush strokes make interesting designs. The three easy-to-copy designs shown here and on page 46 are created primarily with basic painting tools like artist's brushes, texture rollers, and paint pads. The designs range in scale from small to medium to large.

Paint the design on walls rather than use wallcoverings, or paint fabrics for unique accent pillows instead of selecting patterned fabrics. For small accessories, use smaller brushes and shorter brush strokes.

Vary the paint colors, selecting different colors for the different brush strokes. Keep in mind that dark and dull colors tend to recede while bright colors and metallic paints tend to advance. Metallic paints, which reflect light, add drama. For painting on fabrics, use the specialty paints intended for textiles (page 15).

When painting, overlap the brush strokes for a more layered, dimensional look. The spaces between the strokes can be varied slightly for interest. Experiment with the paint colors and techniques before you begin the actual project by painting on a large sheet of cardboard or on a remnant of fabric.

MATERIALS

- ◆ #4 round artist's brush, for small swirled design.
- ◆ #4 fan brush, #2 flat artist's brush, and #4 round artist's brush, for medium swirled design.
- ◆ 3" (7.5 cm) flat paintbrush, texture roller, and #4 round artist's brush, for large swirled design.
- ◆ Craft acrylic paints or fabric paints.
- ◆ Paint tray.

SWIRLED DESIGNS are made with brush
strokes in several colors. These simple designs
may be painted on walls as well as on fabrics.

How to paint a small swirled design

1. Apply the first paint color to surface in slightly curved brush strokes about 4″ (10 cm) long and 4″ to 6″ (10 to 15 cm) apart, using #4 round artist's brush. Allow to dry.

2. Apply second color in curving brush strokes about 1½″ (3.8 cm) long, using same brush; use less pressure on paintbrush so strokes are not as wide. Allow some strokes to overlap those of first color. Allow to dry.

3. Apply third color in curving strokes about 1″ (2.5 cm) long, using tip of same brush. Allow some strokes to overlap the first color.

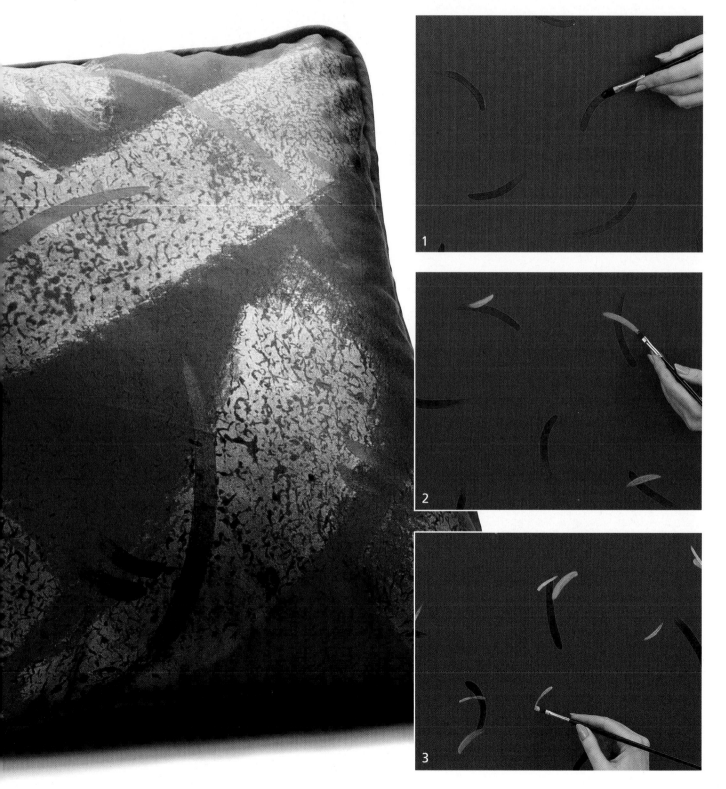

How to paint a medium swirled design

1. Apply first paint color to surface in brush strokes about 4" (10 cm) long, using fan brush. Allow to dry.

2. Apply the second color through middle of the first color in brush strokes about 6" (15 cm) long, using #2 flat artist's brush; vary the position for added interest. Allow to dry.

3. Apply third color in slightly curved brush strokes about 1½" to 2" (3.8 to 5 cm) long, using #4 round artist's brush. Allow to dry.

4. Wet the fan brush; blot on paper towel. Separate the bristles into small fingers. Dip into fourth paint color ¼" (6 mm), keeping bristles separated. Apply to surface in short brush strokes, about 1" (2.5 cm) long, applying light pressure.

How to paint a large swirled design

1. Dilute first paint color, one part paint to two parts water. Using 3" (7.5 cm) paintbrush, apply paint to surface in slightly curved brush strokes, from 7" to 14" (18 to 35.5 cm) long. Allow to dry.

2. Dilute second paint color, one part paint to one part water; spread a thin layer in paint tray. Apply paint to texture roller; blot onto paper, then roll onto surface, overlapping the brush strokes from step 1. Allow to dry.

3. Apply the third color in curving brush strokes about 6" to 12" (15 to 30.5 cm) long, using #4 round artist's brush; overlap the brush strokes from step 1. Allow to dry.

4. Apply fourth color in pairs of short brush strokes, using #4 round artist's brush; overlap the edges of the strokes from step 1.

ABOVE: STENCILED TILES of this table-top were painted with ceramic paint. The ceramic paints were then heat-hardened before the ceramic tiles were installed.

LEFT: FAUX ONYX LAMP was painted with a primer recommended for use on glossy surfaces, then painted with a faux onyx finish, using craft acrylic paint.

Painting Ceramics

Glazed ceramics can be hand-painted to coordinate with the decorating scheme of a room. In order to paint on ceramics, it is important that you either prepare the surface by applying a primer recommended for glossy surfaces or that you use the specialty paints designed for ceramic painting. With either method, there is no need to sand the surface to degloss it before painting.

If you use a primer recommended for glossy surfaces, such as a stain-killing primer (page 9), the ceramic piece may be painted using latex or craft acrylic paint; glossy paints are recommended if you want to retain the sheen of glazed ceramic. The paint adheres well to the ceramic, provided the correct primer is used.

For another method of painting ceramics, use one of the ceramic paints that can be applied directly to the glazed ceramic without the use of a primer. These water-based paints, such as Liquitex® Glossies™ and DEKA®-Gloss, are heat-hardened in a low-temperature oven to further improve the ceramic paint's durability, adhesion, and water resistance.

Ceramic paints produce a hand-painted look, often with an uneven coverage that becomes part of the unique character of each piece. They vary in transparency, and some are easier to work with if they are thinned; for maximum durability, dilute the paints with a clear paint medium that is designed for use with ceramic paint. You may also want to spread the paints thinly, allowing the brush strokes to show, to emphasize the hand-painted quality of the design.

Use ceramic paints for display items, such as vases or decorative plates. Although ceramic paints are nontoxic, they are not recommended for use on eating or drinking utensils where food will come into contact with the paint. For best results, hand wash the painted ceramics in lukewarm water with mild detergent.

Two methods for painting glazed ceramics

A

PRIMER AND LATEX OR CRAFT ACRYLIC PAINT METHOD (A). Apply a primer that is recommended for glossy surfaces; allow to dry. Paint over the primer, using latex or craft acrylic paint; any of the painting techniques recommended for latex or craft acrylic paint can be used.

CERAMIC PAINT METHOD (B). Use ceramic paint, applying it directly to glazed ceramic surface; use desired painting technique, such as stenciling. Allow to dry. Heat-harden the paint in a low-temperature oven, following the manufacturer's directions.

B

More ideas for painting ceramics

TOP, RIGHT: COLOR-WASHED CERAMIC TEAPOT was painted with a fan brush. To achieve this effect, apply ceramic paint sparingly in cross-hatching brush strokes.

TOP, LEFT: SWIRLED DESIGNS (page 45) accent clear glass votives and a coordinating napkin ring. Ceramic paints were used for this technique.

LEFT: OLD CANISTERS are given a new look by painting them with a primer suitable for glossy surfaces, then with latex paint. Easy freehand designs (page 42) add a cheerful touch.

ABOVE: GOLD METALLIC DESIGN is painted on the wall at the head of the bed. Small fleur-de-lis motifs painted randomly on the walls support the decorating theme.

LEFT: SYMMETRICALLY DESIGNED GREEK COLUMNS painted on the wall visually support the shelf. The swag and tassel border is painted at picture-rail level.

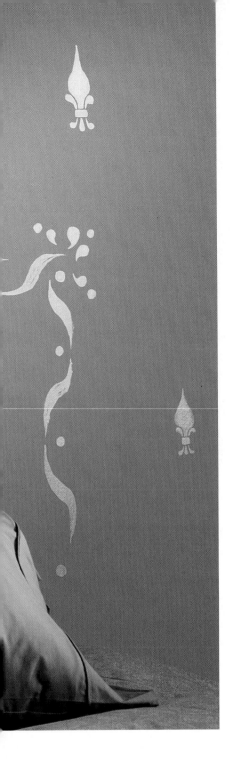

Freehand Painted Designs for Walls

Freehand painting is a speedy way to add eye-catching interest to plain painted walls. Designs can range from stately architectural details to fanciful motifs. Simple symmetrical designs in one color are easiest to paint, while asymmetrical designs or designs with multiple colors may take a little preplanning. Use some of the designs shown here, or look for inspiration in wallpaper patterns, clip-art books, or stencils.

Craft acrylic paints or latex wall paints can be used for freehand painting. Acrylic paints, available in smaller quantities, may be more economical, depending on the size of the project. If a paint color is mixed, be sure to mix enough paint ahead of time to complete the entire project. Use wide, flat paintbrushes to paint bold lines; use other artist's brushes in styles and sizes necessary to achieve the desired look.

Allow the painted designs to be imperfect; that is part of the charm of freehand painting. To gain confidence, practice designs on tagboard or craft paper taped to the wall with masking tape.

MATERIALS

- ◆ Craft acrylic paint or latex wall paint.
- ◆ Paintbrushes in desired sizes and styles.
- ◆ Masking tape.
- ◆ Yardstick or carpenter's level, for marking guides as necessary.

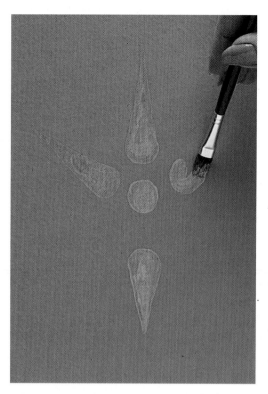

SYMMETRICAL MOTIFS. Paint the center of the design first; then paint small sections of the design on either side of the center, working outward until entire design is complete.

BORDERS. Mark guide points on wall, using yardstick or carpenter's level, before painting evenly spaced swags or wavy lines. Keep the brush moving at a constant, rhythmic pace across the wall, redipping brush in paint as necessary. Fill in details after entire border is laid out.

LARGE DESIGNS. Mark faint pencil guidelines on the wall at strategic points in large designs. Paint dominant details first to anchor design on wall; then paint secondary design lines to complete design.

RANDOM MOTIFS. Mark placement for motifs, using small pieces of masking tape, before beginning to paint. Vary sizes or colors for added interest, if desired.

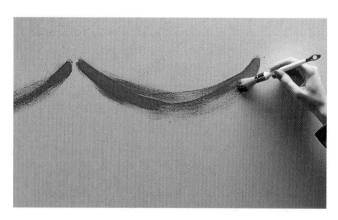

More ideas for freehand designs

RIGHT: CONTEMPORARY ASYMMET-RICAL DESIGN painted on the wall boldly outlines a window. Small motifs taken from the design are painted randomly on the wall, unifying the room.

BELOW: FAUX BRICKWORK painted on the wall under a shelf resembles a fireplace and mantel. Faux brickwork chair rail continues around the room.

Continued

More ideas for freehand designs
(CONTINUED)

PAINT different designs in each section of the legs of a table or the turned posts of a headboard.

OPPOSITE: BRIGHTLY PAINTED TABLE
is a cheerful accent for a child's room.

ABOVE: HEADBOARD is creatively painted for a personalized, whimsical effect.

BELOW: CERAMIC PAINTS are used to
create a one-of-a-kind decorative bowl.

MARK a grid onto the sur-
face, using a pencil; paint
along the lines, using a liner
brush. Fill in the areas with
a random, light application
of paint.

Continued

More ideas for freehand designs
(CONTINUED)

UNFINISHED MEDICINE CABINETS,
available at unpainted-furniture stores, can be
decoratively painted with stylized designs.

ABOVE: WALL DISPLAY features a shelf with freehand designs and stenciled wall designs. The ceramics are decorated with freehand designs combined with sponge painting; specialty ceramic paints were used.

BELOW: WOODEN STOOL is given new life with painted leaf designs.

TRACE around simple patterns, using a pencil. Fill in the areas with paint; allow to dry. Then add details with contrasting colors.

Hand-painted Trompe l'Oeil

Sophisticated trompe l'oeil murals have the ability to create visual space, almost to the extent that the viewer is tempted to walk into the scene. Such a level of sophistication, obtained by few artists, requires intense study and practice.

There are, however, some simple trompe l'oeil effects that can be successfully achieved with a less skillful hand. The success of the illusion depends on a few basic principles, including scale, perspective, and shading.

SCALE

Objects must be painted the size they would normally appear. Objects look smaller the farther away they are. If an image is to be viewed at close range, it should be painted life-size.

PERSPECTIVE

A sense of depth and distance can be developed by painting images in perspective. In a simple one-point perspective drawing, parallel horizontal lines that run from foreground to background seem to converge at a point on the horizon called the vanishing point.

SHADING

Determine an imaginary light source, and add highlights and shadows to the painted images in reference to that light. For simple trompe l'oeil effects, paint each object in one color tone. Then add highlights by mixing white paint into that color. Paint shadows within the objects by mixing black paint into the original color. Shadows around objects should be painted by mixing black into the original color of the background. It is helpful to study still life photographs to determine the placement of highlights and shadows.

MATERIALS

- Drawing paper, pencil, ruler.
- Graphite paper.
- Craft acrylic paints in desired colors; white paint for mixing highlight

colors; black paint for mixing shadow colors.
- Artist's brushes, such as a flat shader and a liner.

How to draw an image in one-point perspective

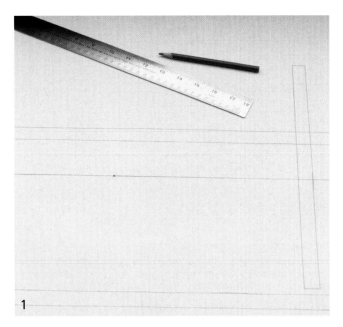

1

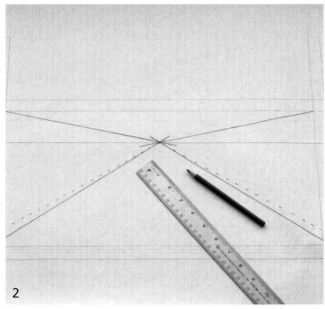

2

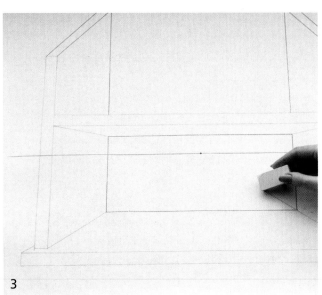

3

4

1. Draw a horizontal line (red) across the paper to represent the horizon, or eye level. Draw a point on the horizon to represent vanishing point. Draw to scale primary vertical and horizontal lines (blue) in the foreground, placing horizontal lines a distance above or below the horizon equal to the actual distance they would appear above or below eye level.

2. Draw lines (blue) to represent all parallel horizontal lines that run from the foreground to the background, beginning each line in the foreground and converging all lines at the vanishing point. (Dotted lines show extension of converging parallel lines to vanishing point.)

3. Draw horizontal lines in the background, parallel to horizon line. Draw vertical lines in background. Draw any other connecting lines from foreground to background. Erase unnecessary lines to avoid confusion.

4. Add detail lines and round corners as desired. Erase any unnecessary lines.

How to paint a simple trompe l'oeil image

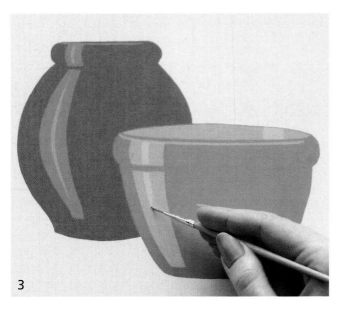

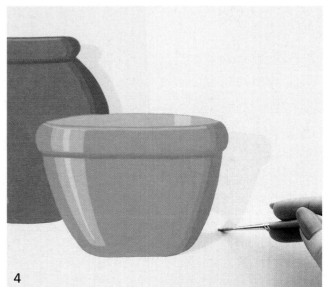

1. Prepare surface (page 9). Apply base coat of the desired color. Allow to dry. Draw the image as in steps 1 to 4, opposite. Or, copy life-size images from magazines. Transfer the image to the surface, using graphite paper.

2. Paint image in single color tones, using desired artist's brushes. Allow to dry. Redraw detail lines.

3. Mix lighter shades of each color, by adding white paint. Paint highlights in areas that would be in direct line with imaginary light source. Allow to dry.

4. Mix darker shades of each color, by adding black paint. Paint shadows that would be created if imaginary light source was shining on image.

Trompe l'Oeil Stenciling

For people who are less confident of their freehand painting skills or would simply like to try another avenue, a trompe l'oeil effect can be created with stencils. There are some high-quality precut stencils available, with multiple overlays that help the artist create realistic, life-size images. With the use of shading and highlighting techniques, the artist is able to add depth and perspective, giving the stenciled images visual dimension.

Some of the more realistic stencils do not have the bridges, or blank spaces, so common with most stencils. Pinpoint registration marks ensure that each overlay lines up exactly over the preceding one. A pouncing method of application, using craft acrylic paints, allows for successful blending of colors and shading. A wide selection of stencil brushes allows the artist to use a different brush for each paint color, in sizes proportionate to the sizes of the stencil openings. Masking tape wrapped around the bristles ¼" (6 mm) from the end helps support the bristles during the pouncing motion.

Follow the manufacturer's instructions and color suggestions for completing the stencil, or select color combinations as desired. Several colors may be applied with each overlay, depending on the complexity of the design. Each opening may receive a base color, applied in gradation shading, and then another color for darker shading in areas that would appear in shadow. As with other trompe l'oeil methods, determine an imaginary light source, highlighting foreground areas that would be in direct line with that light source and shading areas that would appear in shadow. After completing the stenciled image, add the shadow that the image would cast on the surface behind it.

MATERIALS

- Precut stencil with multiple overlays.
- Painter's masking tape.
- Craft acrylic paints.
- Stencil brushes.
- Disposable plates; paper towels.

How to stencil a trompe l'oeil image

1. Position the first overlay as desired; secure to the surface, using painter's masking tape. Mark the surface through registration holes, using sharp pencil.

2. Place 1 to 2 tsp. (5 to 10 mL) of paint on disposable plate. Apply masking tape around bristles, ¼" (6 mm) from the end. Dip tip of stencil brush into paint. Using circular motion, blot brush onto folded paper towel until bristles are almost dry.

3. Hold the brush perpendicular to the surface, and apply paint to the first opening, using up-and-down pouncing motion. Apply the paint lightly and evenly throughout the entire opening.

4. Deepen color to desired level by repeated pouncing in areas of the opening that would not be highlighted, shading darker into areas that would appear in shadow; leave highlighted areas pale.

5

6

7

5. Repeat steps 3 and 4 for all openings that receive the same color. Repeat step 2 with the shading color and another brush. Apply shading to areas of openings that would appear in shadow.

6. Repeat steps 2 to 5 for any additional colors on the first overlay. Remove overlay.

7. Position second overlay, aligning registration marks; tape to surface. Repeat steps 2 to 6 for second overlay. Repeat for any subsequent overlays until image is complete.

8. Follow step 2, opposite, using small stencil brush and gray or brown paint. Apply the paint lightly with a pouncing motion along the edges of image opposite light source, simulating shadows.

8

More ideas for trompe l'oeil effects

ABOVE: RAISED PANELS are painted on an interior door, using precut stencils as a guide. Chair rail molding is an illusion created with trompe l'oeil stenciling.

MARK the placement for each panel on door. Move the stencil up or down to complete each panel. Follow the principle of shading (page 53) to determine dark and light areas.

RIGHT: RECESSED NOOK painted in freehand trompe l'oeil invites visitors to take a second look.

BELOW: WINDOW is painted in freehand trompe l'oeil, using one-point perspective (page 53). Stenciled flowers and greens suggest an outdoor flower bed.

Faux Mosaic

Simulate a mosaic design with a painting technique that uses small pieces of sponge as stamps. For easier handling, several pieces of sponge are glued to a small piece of foam board, allowing you to create intricate stamped designs in a single printing. Make a separate stamp for each mosaic design and each color because the stamps cannot be cleaned. If the project is not finished in one day, used stamps may be kept overnight in tightly sealed plastic bags.

Faux mosaic works for smooth or textured surfaces. Use it to create a border design along the ceiling, to frame a window or archway, or to embellish the wall below a chair rail. Or use faux mosaic on accessories like vases and planter stands.

Before you start painting, you may want to sketch the mosaic design to scale on graph paper as shown on page 33.

MATERIALS

- Flat or low-luster latex paint, for base coat.

- Latex or craft acrylic paints in desired colors, for mosaic design.

- Cellulose sponges; slightly dampened sponges are easier to use.

- Pieces of foam board; craft glue; disposable plates; artist's eraser.

- Utility knife or razor blade; ruler.

- Carpenter's level, for marking walls.

- Transparent Mylar® sheets and painter's masking tape.

How to make the stamps for a mosaic design

1. Cut the cellulose sponge into ¾" (2 cm) squares or other mosaic shapes, using a utility knife.

2. Cut piece of foam board with a utility knife, to be used as a base for the stamp. For an overall grid design, cut 2" × 2" (5 × 5 cm) base to hold four ¾" (2 cm) sponge squares. For a straight-line design, cut 1" × 4" (2.5 × 10 cm) base to hold four sponges. For small details, cut a 1" × 1" (2.5 × 2.5 cm) base to hold one sponge.

3. Glue sponges of same height to base, spacing them about ⅛" (3 mm) apart. To keep mosaic design irregular in appearance, do not space sponges precisely. Allow glue to dry.

4. Make stamps for mosaic motifs by cutting desired shape from foam board, for base. Cut the sponges into desired shapes to fill the design area; glue pieces to base, spacing them about ⅛" (3 mm) apart. Allow glue to dry.

How to paint a faux mosaic design

1. Measure area to be painted with mosaic design. Make diagram of the area on graph paper, drawing the mosaic design to scale on the diagram, using colored pencils; include any details such as motifs or borders.

2. Apply base coat to wall in the desired color; use a mortar color for base coat, for the look of real grout. Allow to dry.

Continued

How to paint a faux mosaic design
(CONTINUED)

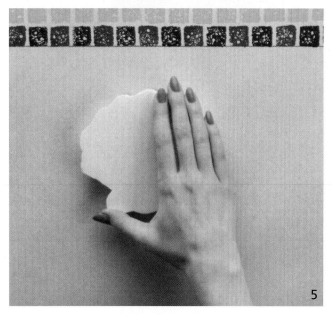

3. Mark outer guidelines of the design area lightly on base-coated surface, using a pencil; to mark walls, use carpenter's level. Mark any other significant placement lines, such as dividing lines, borders, and motifs.

4. Pour small amount of latex or craft acrylic paint in each color for mosaic stamps onto disposable plates. Dip stamp lightly into paint for a one-color stamp (A). Or apply paint colors to individual pieces of sponge (B). Blot onto paper to remove excess paint.

5. Stamp the mosaic design onto surface, using marked lines as a guide, stamping any dividing lines, borders, and motifs; reapply paint to the stamp as necessary. Use a separate stamp for each mosaic design and color combination.

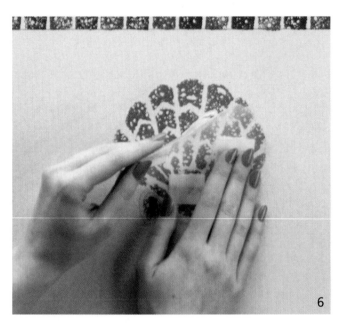

6. Cut Mylar® for each motif, 1/8″ (3 mm) larger on all sides. Secure folded painter's masking tape to back of Mylar. Mask off stamped motifs by securing Mylar to the surface over the motif.

7. Finish stamping background area. When stamping the area surrounding motifs, allow the stamps to overlap the Mylar. Allow paint to dry.

8. Remove the Mylar from motif areas. Erase any marked lines that are not covered with paint, using artist's eraser.

Index